INTEGRATED CONFLICT MANAGEMENT FOR MANAGERS- THEORY AND PRACTICE

Subramanian.K MBA, Ph.D.

Published by

Centre for Conflict Management Studies

India

2020

PREFACE

A necessary part of learning management in these days is learning about the conditions under which people can be motivated to perform work in organisations despite the conflicts and or create a better conflict situation/level to enhance the performance constructively. Effectiveness of managers depends on how well they understand the underlying dynamics of the conflict, which may be all together different from its expression, and whether they can identify the crucial tactical points for intervention. This is the challenge of Conflict management.

This book is one of the resultants of a series of studies to attempt to understand the greater world of conflict and its management among business organisations. There exists a dearth of literature directly dealing and pertaining to the field of conflict management in India. This book address the research gaps in theorising conflict management by exploring various theories, models and assumptions, thereby synchronising and presenting before the reader. Learned academicians and practitioners will certainly feel informed and substantially gained when and only when conflict management theories are presented in a synthesised manner. This is an attempt to bring forth the forte of conflict management theories and models. This work also postulate integrated models and explore suggestive scenarios. I am sure this will be beneficial for executives, managerial workforce, business consultants, academicians and policy makers.

Acknowledgement of help is the most pleasant and pious of all tasks for any author. At the same time, at least I am finding myself captive of trepidation that the naughty absence of mind may play blight sport to send the kindness of helping souls to the boundary of forgetting. The apprehension is real and is beyond my control to address. Happily, even the worst of cluttered memories fails to eclipse some outstanding acts of generosity.

Whether I need to thank the fruit for it gave its taste when I was in great need of it, or the branch which sustained the fruit or the twigs or the tree or the root or the seed or the soil or the earth? I thank the exponential reality we may experience through the creative explorations, sustainable reinventions and the creative destructions when we say we are living. Probably that is how I am in receipt of few glimpses of the essence of old, yet matchless word-GOD.

I intend to dedicate this work to those unsung and forgotten heroes- *odorous orphans* who experienced the essence of management with its most beautiful rainbows. Some of them are still underrepresented and consciously ignored by modern management thinkers and practitioners. Those unsung heroes are part of a *grand plan* to give the simple solutions to our complex conflicts. When we receive the answers as simple as they can be from those Mahatmas, we may reassure that they are coming out directly from God to the humanity. I heard some of it from the likes of life and works of Mahatma Gandhi, *uncommonness in few common men* and attempting to express so as to be in this world upon. Voices of eternal truth from those great souls will certainly be constant motivations as like the grand banyan tree representing the creating, nourishing, sustaining and integrating principles that elevate human beings to higher non-dual consciousness.

I wish a great success to YOU the preader for considering this research work robust enough to attempt to examine.

K.SUBRAMANIAN

TABLE OF CONTENTS

The Latin word *conflictus*, as "striking together with force" implies disagreement, discord, and friction among the members of a group. It indicates those interactions in which words, emotions, and actions "strike together" to produce disruptive effects. Conflict has been defined in many ways depending upon the suitability, focus and group interest. Some conflicts are characterised as intrapersonal, while others have been described as interpersonal. Some manifestations of conflict have also been recognised in the organisational context.

As it emerges mainly between two groups, conflict is characterised in terms of overall group interest and union-management conflict has been popular term particularly coined to describe similar phenomena in different organisations. Although there are many definitions available in the literature, it is necessary to restrict ourselves to definitions that best describe organisational conflict with emphasis on managerial sphere. A sample of definitions describing varying manifestations of conflict in organisations are quoted below-

- "Conflict is a breakdown in the standard mechanism of decision-making, so that an individual or a group experiences difficulty in selecting an action alternative" (March and Simon, 1958).This definition views the organisation primarily as a decision making body, whereas all agents are engaged in making big or small decisions. Conflict occurs when the parties do not agree on which alternative should be chosen for implementation. The scope of this definition is more or less confined to the decision-making process.

- "Conflict is a struggle of values, or claims to status, power and scarce resources in which the aims of the conflicting parties are not only to gain desired values but also to neutralise or injure or eliminate their rivals" (Coser, 1967). Although conflicts do arise from the factors such as values, power and status, there are a host of other factors that are as potent. In that sense, Coser's definition seems to be more limited and more appropriate to the general social context.

- "A situation in which the conditions, practices or goals for the different participants, are inherently incompatible" (Smith, 1966.p.511). "Conflict is described as a resultant of antecedent conditions, affective states of the individuals involved, cognitive states of the individuals and conflictual behaviour ranging from positive resistance to overt aggression" (Pondy, 1967). Pondy has mentioned four stages of conflict and distinguished a conflict aftermath which means that if the conflict is not resolved to the satisfaction of the parties, the basis for more conflict may be established. These two definitions in question are quite wide and embrace both the process and the structural aspects of the conflict.

- "Conflict is viewed as the active striving for one's own preferred outcome which, if attained, precludes the attainment by others of their own preferred outcome, thereby producing hostility" (Likert and Likert, 1976). Conflict occurs when party forces its views over others to see that their preferred outcomes are achieved. Here the needs and the personalities are actively involved. Conflicts are seen to be unidirectional in that one party strives without caring the outcome or the end result. The scope of this definition seems to be rather limited.

- "Some type of incompatibility, one goal stands in the way of another…further conflict can be seen as the expression of objective, structural dichotomy especially of the asymmetrical relationships" (Galtung, 1992.p.2)

- "A conflict is brought about between two or more parties when they perceive incompatible goals, scarce rewards, and interference in achieving the goals" (Folger & Poole, 1984).

- "A situation or state between at least two interdependent parties, which characterised by perceived differences that the parties evaluate as negative. This often results in negative emotional states and behaviours intended to overcome the opposition" (Katz & Lawyer, 1993, p.7).

- "A feature of normal and frequently collaborative and creative relationships, an integral part of competitive system… conflicts… are deeply-rooted in human needs, and… frequently require major environmental and policy restructuring for their resolution" (Burton,1990,p.1).

- "The process that begins when one party perceives that the other party has negatively affected something that he or she cares about" (Thomas, 1992, p.653).

- "An interactive process manifested in incompatibility, disagreement, or dissonance within or between social entities (i.e., individual, group, organisation, etc)" (Rahim, 1992.p.16).

- "Conflict occurs as incompatibility of behaviours, cognitions and/or affect among the individuals or groups that may lead to aggressive expression of social incompatibility" (Boardman and Horowitz, 1994).

1.1 CONFLICT POTENTIAL AND ORGANISATIONAL LEVELS

In a theoretical perspective, the potential for the conflicts to occur in every organisational level is alarmingly high. The historical importance attached to the conflicts at the interpersonal levels/individual levels alone may not bring the desired results in these days. The better we understand the potentials for the conflict in all the organisational levels the better we can frame a decent mechanism to cope up with those situations. Although it has been widely acclaimed that a conflict arises in one level can spawn or moves to another or other levels and vice versa.

1.1.1 Individual group member

A group member/team member experiences the constant intra-psychological struggles and conflicts and he express these externally for he seeks to cooperate with the other team members. The known conflict mechanisms in this context usually appear within individuals and corrupt their perceptions, thinking, feelings and their external behaviour. The perception capability of the individual can be strongly impaired through the effects of stress, tension and pressure. The result can lead to selective or distorted perception or even the fading out of perceptions that do not conform to the preconceived picture. This is how prejudices occur and become fixed, since all evidence, which might contradict previous perceptions, are suppressed and discarded. The concepts and ideas which people form on the basis of such distorted perceptions are likely to become into one-sided black and white pictures, which can no longer easily corrected by further evidence or perceptions. The members take only information that confirms the prejudice. In the emotional sector, empathy dries up. People become encapsulated one from another, prisoner of their own feelings. Sympathy and antipathy serve to create a polarised emotional picture. If the conflict escalates, the picture seems to be more dramatic as all point of reference to the outside world is lost. Unconscious or semiconscious driving forces and motives become dominant in those situations. Perceiving, thinking and willing all mutually reinforce one another in a vicious spiral and the tension can be even more difficult when they contradict each other. In the external behaviour of these individuals, a noticeable change will preoccupy. Stereotypes, rumor spreading and compulsiveness control their actions.

1.1.2 The interaction or psychosocial level

Each group will need to organise itself around certain roles if it is to achieve its goals and also to maintain cohesion as a team. Conflicts tend to occur when a group member –

- Feels pressure from the group to assume a role in which he does not want and to which he/other members objects the same or vice versa
- Experiences the allocated roles as constraining and decelerating his development
- Feel avoidance / covert sanctions imposed by other elements of a team
- Hierarchical constraints, especially the leadership dilemmas and formal/informal authority.

1.1.3 The content or the issue level

Rational individuals often assume that conflicts arise and keep it as long as everybody remains objective. However, as a conflict escalates, issue related and psycho-social issues become increasingly mixed. Potential for conflict can be easily arise at this level if managers fail to recognise that any issue can be perceived and asserted differently by different task groups/team members. Unfortunately, concepts can only rarely be clarified to everyone's satisfaction. The result would be misunderstandings and misinterpretations. There may be a failure to identify the real issues thus producing conflicts.

1.1.4 The procedural / method level

Teams in the organisations are expected to learn and familiarise themselves with a variety of working procedures and methods and must become good at reaching right decisions. Conflicts are often initially experienced as relation-specific, even though the problems can actually be traced to a poor selection of work methods.

1.1.5 External relations and outreach

The relations between a team and its organisational setting can also contain many seeds of conflict. One important aspect is to specify the degree of participation of the team in defining itself against higher-ranking levels or other teams within the organisation. In that sense the extraneous variables for the organisation and its prominent impact on the team members shall play a key role in defining the conflict potentials. These extraneous factors include the social, economic, cultural, political, industrial, technical and other superfluous dimensions that instill the dynamics of change or at least a positional alteration in the organisational setup. External relations and its influences are multitudinal and calls for a holistic and expanded study of conflict potentials. Interestingly, this seems to be the most damaging type of conflicts which are of innumerable in characteristics yet not been able to make positions of.

1.2 PERSPECTIVES ON ORGANISATIONAL CONFLICTS AND ITS MANAGEMENT

The complex variables of conflict fabric had historically initiated the managerial thinkers to formulate a decent idea with which the practicing managers can approach the conflict situation and act upon. Fortunately or unfortunately the perspectives on organisational conflict among the theoretical exponents reflected the ever undergoing process regarding the management of the conflict affairs. Three distinguishable perspectives emerged out of the managerial interactions with the conflict associations and they are interestingly complementary towards each other in certain proportions.

1.2.1 Traditional (unitary) perspectives

This perspective holds that conflict represents a malfunction within the individual, group, department or the organisation. Within it, conflict is seen as bad and harmful and hence should be avoided if possible and eradicated if it erupts .This perspective is called traditional because it has its roots in the Hawthorne studies which were conducted in the United States in the 1924-32 period. It is also referred to as unitary because of its endorsement by managerial thinkers of pre 1970's including Elton Mayo, Dalton, Barrett and Cosier among others. Organisation as a fundamentally harmonious, cooperative structure where no systematic conflict of interest occurs seems to be at the core that lies beneath in this perspective. Common goals are assumed and organisational success or failure is seen as leading to success or failure for the entire human elements that are present in that organisation. Managers are advised by this perspective to see their organisation as analogous to teams with all the team members striving towards the achievement of common goals. The concept of the 'pulling together in the same direction' and that of the 'espirit de corps' are followed unquestioningly and in a flattened view of the same preferences, values beliefs and attitude predispositioned among the human workforce.

Explaining conflict from unitary perspective is difficult rather problematic because, as all the members of the organisation are held to share common objectives and values which unite them; while managerial prerogative is accepted with unified authority and there is organisational loyalty; perhaps too much that a manager has to assume to apply this perspective in the real situation. The unitary perspective sees consensus especially the non conflict in essence as the ideal and natural state. When conflict occurs its existence tends to be explained in one of three ways. Most commonly it is attributed to poor communication. Management accepts responsibility for failing to get its intended message through to its employees and to meet their needs and aspirations.

Conflict is thus seen as being caused by misunderstandings. The instability which led to the conflict breaking out is held to be the result of a lack of trust, openness and adequate communications which are necessarily to be rectified. In other ways, conflict may be seen as a failure by management to design an organisational structure that allows individuals, units or departments to cooperate to achieve organisational objectives. In the third dimension, management may claim that it has shown the workforce the right perspective and that was irreparably sabotaged by a few unrepresented minorities that are essentially unwanted in the workforce, hence the conflict propels as the outcome. Irrespective of which of the three explanations is adopted by the practicing manager the core issues that are advocated to act upon remains the same, eliminating the causes of the conflicts and to reestablish the satisfactory situation that was prevailing in the organisation. The traditional perspective is viewed as the resultant of the historical conflict that was visible throughout the industrial revolution and its immediate aftermath in every economy ranging from European to the Latin American. The class warfare and the industrial schools had their influence on shaping the unitary thoughts which seems to be highly flattened by its own wishes to remain encircled by insulating the changed scenarios.

1.2.2 Pluralist perspectives

It may be noted that the glimpses of this perspective was early identified by many managerial thinkers but the promulgation of pluralist perspective starts with Alan Fox(1966) in United States, an old advocate of unitarian conflict thinker later aloofed himself from the pitfalls of traditional viewpoints. It is called pluralist because it rejects the view that individual employees have the same interests as the management on the other hand and that an organisation is best seen as one big team on the other. Instead it holds that individuals have unique and different interests that they form into cliques on the basis of these and that an organisation is best seen as consisting of many separate but related interest camps each pursuing their own objectives. If however the interests coincide or rather collide whilst others they will clash and the frictional basis can develop into the conflict envisaged. The obvious clashes may be between or among the organisational workforce in every level possible. The contributory expansion of this perspective attained was that it recognised a fact that the conflict may not necessarily among the two parties in the organisation; even more the disagreement among three or more parties in the organisational sphere was visualised and deemed to be imperative in determining the detrimental value of the conflicts. The job of the management becomes one of keeping the balance between potentially conflicting goals and managing the differences between the differing interest groups.

Acceptance of the pluralist perspective implies that conflict is inevitable. Indeed given the organisational relationships, it will be endemic. However unlike the traditional perspective which sees conflict as harmful and something to be eliminated, in the pluralistic view conflict should be accepted since in certain circumstances it may even enhance the relationships and promote the organisational efficiency. Underlying the pluralist perspective ids the belief that conflict can be resolved through compromise to the benefit of all. However it requires all parties to limit their claims to a level which is at least tolerable to the others and which allows further collaboration to continue. Lewis Pondy (1967, p.320) wrote that, "Conflict is not necessarily good or bad, but must be evaluated in terms of its individual organisational functions and dysfunctions. In general, conflict generates pressure to reduce conflict, but chronic conflict persists and is endured under certain conditions and consciously created and managed by the politically astute administrator". For the pluralist the organisation is indeed a system of interrelationships between the individuals and groups within it each pursuing their own goals. Conflicts in an organisation acts as the safety-valve and keeps the organisational elements responsible and even responsive to the internal and external changes. The inevitable conflict has to be managed so that organisational goals are reconciled with the group interests to the benefit of organisational prosperity.

1.2.3 Interactionist perspectives

The interactionist perspective goes beyond the pluralist school's toleration and the management of the conflict. It actually in a way promotes a healthy conflict level by stimulating the conflict situation advocating conscious organisational interventions. It encourages the conflict stimulation and conflict resolution in equal ways. This perspective argues that an individual, group or department that seems to be too peaceful harmonious and or cooperative in some cases can become apathetic and unresponsive to the changing needs. Such extreme cohesion, be it blossoming from an individual thought or that from a group can lead to the stagnation phenomenon that are visibly disconcerted by any changes encouraging a reactionary shield of opposing every change and leniency towards maintaining the status quo would not be a sought-after measure for the organisational set up.

The interactionist view recognises that the conflict occurs as a process or sequence of events. These events take place in conflict episodes between the parties. Whenever the interactions happen, there exist a wider scope for conflict and its management of the same in organisational context was highly appreciated by this perspective. The process of conflict does not occur in a vacuum. Rather they are shaped by structural parameters of the system, the relatively fixed or slow changing conditions influencing events at the interface between the parties. These structural conditions include the properties of the parties as well as the context in which they interact. Most organisational conflicts are managed primarily by the principal parties of the conflict. However one or more third parties may also play a role in managing the conflict. Depending on the system and the interface where the conflict occurs, the third party could be a manager, board of directors, consultant or a mediator etc. The interventions that are exercised by the third parties and subsequent changes in the interrelationship scenario is identified and recognised in the interactionist perspective. The unwinding of the negative outlook regarding the conflicts and to give a more pragmatic vision towards dealing the conflicts in the organisation seems to be the major intransigent force though it was really propelled by the interactionist view.

1.3 FUNCTIONAL AND DYSFUNCTIONAL ASPECTS OF CONFLICT AND ITS MANAGEMENT

The perspectives on organisational conflicts seem to differ in terms of their evaluation of conflict with regard to its functionality aspects. The traditional view sees all conflict as bad, while the pluralist and interactionist perspectives hold that certain conflicts can be good. In other words whether a conflict is functional or disturbs the smooth functioning of the organisational workings is put under litmus test. From 1970's the basic question that arises among the managerial exponents regarding the functional and or dysfunctional aspects of the conflicts are addressed constructively in these days. It has been suggested that under some situations conflict can generate positive response in the organisation. Thus a conflict may have both positive and negative aspects. Boulding has recognised that some optimum level and associated personal stress and tension are necessary for progress and productivity but he portrays conflict primarily as a potential social cost.

Similarly Kahn and others view that one might well make a case for interpreting some conflict as essential for the continued development of mature and competent human beings and they feel that conflict is necessarily a social cost. It has been widely acclaimed as a conflict is functional if it improves the quality of decisions, stimulates creativity and innovation, encourages interest and curiosity amongst the group members, provides a way of airing grievances, releases tensions and encourages self evaluation and change. It is dysfunctional if it breeds discontent, dissolves common ties, leads to the destruction of the group, retards communication, reduces group cohesion, individual interests supplant group goals, reduces group effectiveness and threatens group survival. Functionality is thus defined at the level of the group as a whole in terms of outcomes, rather than in its effects on the individual members. In essence the conflict is functional when it supports the goals of an individual / group /organisation and improves her/his/its performance. It is by this idea amalgamation that functional conflicts are sometimes referred as constructive and or cooperative conflicts. Those conflict situations are regarded as necessarily dysfunctional when it hinders individual's/group's performance towards attaining organisational goals.

1.4 CONFLICT CONTINUUM

Notion and ideas about managing conflict underwent an interesting evolution during the twentieth century among management thinkers. Initially scientific management experts like Frederick Winslow Taylor of United States believed that all conflicts ultimately threaten management's authority and thus had to be avoided or to be quickly resolved. 'Bostonian' Follett, the only leading lady in the whole gamut of management thinkers shifted the spotlight to the man at the centre stage. Perhaps she was the first advocate of constructive conflict practices for the organisation and a dynamic promoter of integration as the leading way for managing the conflicts. Later Elton Mayo and his associates of human relations school recognised the inevitability of conflicts and advised managers to learn to live with it. Emphasis however remained on the resolution of the conflict whenever possible. From the 1970's, organisational experts like, M.A.Rahim, K.W.Thomas, S.P.Robbins among others began to realise that conflicts had both positive and negative outcomes, depending upon its nature and intensity and advocated the balancing views of conflict in the organisations. In addendum to the appreciation of the conflict in its totality a revolutionary idea cropped among the mainstream management thinkers and practitioners that organisations could suffer from too little conflict. Thereafter the intensity of the conflict and its relationship with the outcomes were studied exclusively with a rejuvenated spirit by the exponents of management literature.

Individuals, work groups, departments or organisations that experience too little conflict tend to be plagued by apathy, lack of creativity, indecision and missed work schemas. Excessive conflict, on the other hand, can corrode organisational performance because of in-house fighting, dissatisfaction among the workforce, lack of teamwork, and attrition tendencies. Workplace aggression and active violence can be manifestations of excessive and non productive conflicts. Appropriate types and levels of conflict energise people in more constructive directions. It seems that the conflict continuum advocating a decent conflict energy that is adorable for the organisational performance and it can be directed towards more positive channels by the conscious organisational interventions by the managerial practitioners.

Conflict comes in a variety of forms. Regardless of the form, the essence of conflict seems to be the distortion it causes for the better or the worse in every sphere of organisational life. The vicious circle of conflict is supported and or supplemented by the great potentialities that it inculcates in the organisational development and change clearly indicates that it can give positive returns apart from the usually branded one sided view of its prevarication. Various forms of conflict include the following ones. The fundamental element of every form of conflict seems to be the perceived situation or the initial reactionary means that is exercised by the parties involved in the conflict situation. Conflict has been classified in different ways. Following are the some of the classifications.

2.1 PERCEIVED, LATENT AND MANIFEST CONFLICTS

* Perceived conflicts exist in individuals when they perceive that there is a conflict in the work environment, which may truly be existing or not. Perceived conflict may give rise to real conflict.

* Latent conflicts are one that does not emerge in open i.e. individuals involved in conflict do not show it openly although the conflict exists.

* Manifest conflicts is open conflict where in parties involved in conflict recognise and openly explicitly express the conflict.

2.2 REALISTIC AND NON-REALISTIC CONFLICTS

Realistic conflict arises when participants clash in the pursuit of claims and expectation of gain. It is viewed as a means towards the achievement of specific goals that might be abandoned if other means appear to be more effective. Non-realistic conflict arises from aggressive impulses that seek expression no matter what the object, allows no functional alternative of means. Since it is not aimed at the attainment of concrete results, but at the expression of aggressive impulses in an individual, it draws managerial attention.

2.3 ORGANISED AND UNORGANISED CONFLICTS

Organised and unorganised conflicts exist in organisations. It can be called organised conflict when parties involved in conflict express it in organised manner like strike or lock out, as there are no contraventions of any of the provisions laid down by the organisational framework. Unorganised conflicts are expressed through absenteeism, late coming etc and are essentially system transgressions.

While there are different kinds of conflicts explained above, all conflicts in organisation – both organised and unorganised fall within one of six categories mentioned below–

- External (conflicts related to competition, the marked place, regulation, or on adversarial take over).
- Management process and style (conflicts stemming from leadership style, the decision making process, or organisational structure.
- Strategic direction (conflicts over the company's mission direction, objectives and strategies).
- Operational (conflicts related to issue such as 'quality verses schedule' or 'design-to-production transition').
- Interdepartmental (conflicts that occur when divisions compete with themselves rather than with other companies).
- Value system (conflicts over business philosophy).

2.4 BARGAINING, BUREAUCRATIC AND SYSTEMS CONFLICTS

- Bargaining conflicts occur among the interest groups in competition for scarce resources, this is appropriate for the analysis of labour–management relations, budgeting processes and staff-line conflicts.
- Bureaucratic conflicts between the parties to a superior, subordinate relationship particularly concerned with the problems caused by institutional attempts to control behaviour and the organisations' reaction to such control.
- Systems conflicts occur among parties to a lateral or working relationship or a functional relationship. Analysis of the problems of coordination is the special prefecture of this model.

2.5 ORGANISATIONAL CONFLICTS

Intra-individual, inter personal and inter group conflicts are all inherent in organisational conflicts. The various shades of organisational conflicts are in effect exercise their combined options.

2.5.1 Intrapersonal conflicts

Intrapersonal conflicts occur within an individual, and often involve some form of frustration and or dissonance felt by an individual. Goal, cognitive, affective and role conflicts and ambiguity are common denominations of the intrapersonal conflicts. Frustration occurs when goal-directed behaviour is blocked.

Goal conflicts occur when two or more desired or expected outcomes are seemed and or perceived to be incompatible. Goal conflict may involve inconsistencies between the individual's or group's values and norms and the demands or goals assigned by higher levels in the organisation. More frequently, goal conflict occurs when an individual or group is assigned or selects incompatible goals according to their understanding. The concept of goal difficulty is in fact the essence of goal conflicts. And it refers to the extent to which an individual's or group's goal is at odds with the capacity to achieve the goal. Goal conflict occurs when a goal has either positive and negative features; or when an individual has two or more competing goals thus blocking, one another. Three types of goal conflicts are generally identified.

- *Approach – approach conflict*, where the individual is motivated to approach two or more positive but mutually exclusive goals.
- *Approach – avoidance conflict*, where a single goal has both positive and negative characteristics and individual is motivated to approach and avoid it at the same time. This has relevance to the analysis of organisational behaviour.
- *Avoidance – avoidance conflict*, where the individual is motivated to avoid two or more negative but mutually exclusive goals.

Cognitive conflicts occur when the ideas and thoughts within an individual or between individuals are incompatible. The relative perceptions about the task at hand or the means to achieve the desired results are at the crossroads and the fundamental distortions in the minds of the human elements are vital to be ignored as cognitive dissonance fuels conflicts. Cognitive conflict is sometimes beneficial because it requires teams to engage in activities that are essential to a team's effectiveness. Cognitive conflict focuses attention on assumptions that may underlie a particular issue and which are often ignored. Cognitive conflict improves the quality of team decisions.

Intrapersonal conflicts may also be a consequence of cognitive dissonance, which occurs when individuals recognise inconsistencies in their own thoughts and or behaviour. The existence of substantial and recognised inconsistencies is usually stressful and uncomfortable. Both goal conflict and cognitive conflict causes or triggers the dissonance and accompany many important decision making scenario. The greater the goal conflict before the decision, the greater the cognitive dissonance is likely to be after the decision. The more difficulty individuals have in arriving at the original decision, the greater is their need to justify the decision afterward. Some cognitive dissonances are inevitable as there seems to be a perceptual distinction exists between the actual and the expected world views exercised by the individuals. Cognitive dissonance can fuel role conflict and ambiguity as an individual is expected to play various roles and a clash there from.

The personality mechanism can also be a distinguishable factor that instigates inner conflict among the individuals. Neurotic tendencies are irrational personality mechanisms that an individual uses often unconsciously, which create inner conflict. In turn, inner conflict often results in behaviours that lead to conflict with others. The psychological sources of neurotic tendencies are beyond the scope of discussion but it has been pointed out by many thinkers that neurotic managers might make excessive use of tight organisational controls because they distrust people. A few may be fearful of uncertainty and risk, not just distrustful of others. Those managers may be predisposed to rely on hunches and impressions rather than seek out available facts. Such managers may not use participation and consultation in their decision making unless extremely required to do so. Individuals with neurotic tendencies will always be affected by their cognitive dissonance and usually struggle unsuccessfully with their intrapersonal conflicts. Because they cannot manage their own problems, they often trigger conflict with the others. The excessive distrust and need to control exhibited by neurotic managers is likely trigger conflict with others, especially subordinates who come to feel over controlled and distrusted. Open or covert aggression and hostility will be an out growth creating the vicious circle of conflicts in psycho-social relations of organisational dealings.

Affective conflicts occur when the feelings and emotions within an individual or even between individuals are incompatible. The expressive components as well the intra emotive feelings experienced by every party and its reactionary cognition are important to determine the nature of the conflict in this regard. Affective conflict lowers team effectiveness by provoking hostility, distrust, cynicism, and apathy among team members. Most affective conflicts are focused on personalised anger or resentment, usually directed at specific individuals rather than specific ideas. Affective conflict undermines team effectiveness by preventing teams from engaging in the kinds of activities that are critical to team effectiveness.

*Role conflict*s occur when expectations of a role are materially different or even opposite from the behaviour anticipated by that person in that role. The wings of role conflict have its sway in the intrapersonal level as well as to other levels particularly to the interpersonal level. A role is a set of expectations people have about the behaviour of a person in a position. Such behaviour may be formally prescribed by job description, delegation, organisational manuals, and the likes and is derived from the tasks, missions, procedures, or instructions. Roles may also be derived from the informal activities in which members may be engaged. An individual may feel role conflict because there is no way to meet on expectation without rejecting other. Mutually exclusive expectations may arise from a persons' behaviour in many ways. Some of them can be identified as follows–

- When an individual is asked to do a job for which he is not capable of doing or time and resources are not just sufficient to do the job,
- When an individual is asked to do a job which does not fit with his own value system,
- When an individual receives roles from different sources and if those sources prescribe different behaviour,
- When an individual holds two or more roles and their expectations are different and even mutually exclusive as perceived by that individual.

Normally all those factors which are associated with the determination of role expectations may be responsible for role conflict because role conflict arises due to mutually exclusive role expectations. Role ambiguity, organisational positions, personal characteristics are all contributory channels to the role conflicts amongst the individuals. *Role ambiguity* arises when uncertainty or lack of clarity surrounding expectations about a single role. Like role conflict, severe role ambiguity may cause stress and subsequent coping behaviours. The coping behaviours may includes–aggressive actions and hostile communications, ignoring and conscious avoidance causing withdrawal from the situations and seeking guidance through organisational mechanisms. Research findings are not clear cut on the relationships among the role conflict, role ambiguity, and their outcomes. However they indicate stress reactions, aggression, hostility, and withdrawal among others.

2.5.2 Interpersonal conflicts

Interpersonal conflict arises from personal differences, information deficiency, role incompatibility and environmental stress. It usually involves two or more individuals who believe that their attitudes, behaviours, or preferred goals are in opposition. Many interpersonal conflicts are based on some type of role conflict and or role ambiguity. They may stem out of the intrapersonal levels that precipitates as a visible component through the conflict mechanism.

Inter-psychic conflicts exist within an individual when she or he feels drawn to two or more divergent desires or actions ignited through external situations and activates conflicts at psycho-social levels. Psycho-social conflicts exist between people or between a person and a group or vice versa and is present when a person must choose in favour of one course of action, at the expense of an equally desirable course of action (e.g. personal goals at the expense of groups/organisational goals). Conflict of interest is present when parties involved in conflict share the same understanding of the situation but prefers a different and incompatible solution to problem. Conflict of understanding occurs when parties involved in conflict do not share the same conceptualisation of the situation. This may occur because of divergent ideologies, cultures, values or cognitive structures.

2.5.3 Intragroup conflicts

Intragroup conflict occurs when the actions or beliefs of one or more members of the group are unacceptable to – and hence are resisted by *one or more* of the other group members. Intragroup conflict involves clashes among some or all of the group's members, which often affect the groups' processes and effectiveness. In many instances conflict in a group occurs because members must compete for limited resources. Once the conflict begins, it often intensifies before it begins abate. This conflict spiral is produced by a host of factors, including misperceptions, commitment, entrapment, behavioural provocations, reciprocity, and coalitions.

2.5.4 Intergroup conflicts

Intergroup conflict can be expressed as the behaviour that occurs among organisational groups when participants identify with one group and perceive that other groups may block their group's achievement or expectations. Intergroup conflict requires four ingredients- group identification, observable group differences, competition and frustration. The employees have to perceive themselves as part of an identifiable group or department, the presence of observable difference of some form and the third ingredient of the frustration should be felt by the group members. The element of competition plays an important role and creates the platform to express intergroup conflicts.

Intergroup conflict within organisations can occur horizontally across departments or vertically between different levels of the organisation. Conflict can also occur between different divisions or business units with an organisation. Some of the major sources of intergroup conflict can be identified as goal incompatibility, differentiation, task interdependence and limited resources.

2.5.5 Inter-organisational conflicts

Another visible conflict dominion does exist in the inter-organisational levels where multiple groups from more than one organisation may also be part of the conflict continuum. The groups in the organisations perceive that other groups may block their group's achievement or expectations' conflicts. This is fueled through the organisational aspirations arising from the macro business environment when organisations compete for market share, economical compulsions, business priorities, value promotion or to satisfy organisation's self promotive leniency.

2.6 PROCEDURAL AND STRUCTURAL CONFLICTS

Procedural conflicts occur when people differ over the process to use for managing an organisational *decision- inviting* situation. It can be regarded as the style or the method with which the human elements want to achieve the desired results. The very nature of the structure of an organisation also gives rise to conflict. Modern organisations are not immune to the structural conflicts even though they sometimes incorporate the matrix structure and try to pool logically the available resources through under the project banner. In classical organisation there are several types of structural conflicts as indicated below.

- Hierarchical conflicts – exist between various levels in the hierarchy of the organisation like board of director and top management, middle management with supervising personnel, management vs. workers.
- Functional conflicts – exists between various functional departments in every organisation like marketing, personnel, financial, production etc.
- Line vs staff conflicts – Intra organisational functional experts and other officials may have their conflicts with the line managers who are primarily delegators of the task assigned.
- Formal – informal conflicts exists between formal and informal organisational structure and set up among the workforce.

❏ Diversity- based conflicts can occur because of the differences existing and or felt by the workforce regarding age, gender, religion, caste, traditions and other cultural background.

2.7 INNOVATIVE CONFLICTS

Innovative conflict is the most dramatic form of conflict in complex organisation and has its generous hands in ground-breaking movements that challenge the very legitimacy of the organisation or in some cases, the present anomalies in the organisational structure. This is different from other kinds of conflict that it does not ask for a greater share of the scarce resources but they demand that all the resources be redistributed to new organisation and that the old systems cease to exist.

2.8 HOT AND COLD CONFLICTS

Conflict can be both a cold (cognitive) and a hot (emotional and cognitive) experience (Rahim, 1992.p.17). Cold conflict mainly involves the cognitive experiences of seeking information, examining alternatives, evaluating options, and the deciding between two or more alternatives. In cold conflict, the experience is primarily adult (mature), computational, and without emotion. On the other hand, hot conflict involves a mix of cognitive and emotional experiences within and between conflicting persons that can erupt into hurtful or extremely harmful behaviours by either party. In cold conflict, people are usually considerate, calculating, and well intentioned when they attempt to handle the conflict and to optimise their outcomes. In hot conflict, people are usually angry, frustrated, and sad and may be malicious or even murderous if the dynamics of the conflict go beyond acceptable rational and organisational constraints.

2.9 TASK, RELATIONSHIP AND PROCESS CONFLICTS

Research has shown conflict to be multidimensional (e.g. Amason, 1996; Cosier & Schwenck, 1990; Jehn, 1995; Van de Vliert & De Dreu, 1994). Thus, it is possible for one dimension of conflict to enhance effectiveness whereas another hinders consensus and commitment between group members. Based on past research (Amason & Sapienza, 1997; Cosier & Rose, 1977; Guetzkow & Gyr, 1954; Jehn, 1997; Pelled, 1996; Pinkley, 1990; Wall & Nolan, 1986) conflict in work groups is often categorised into three types – relationship, task, or process conflict and these types have tended to have different effects on team performance.

Numerous studies have investigated the relationships between different types of conflict and several personal, group and organisational outcomes–such as satisfaction, tension or commitment. Task conflict is positively related to the quality of ideas and innovation (West and Anderson, 1996), the increase of constructive debate (Jehn, Northcraft & Neale, 1999), the affective acceptance of group decisions (Amason, 1996), or the prevention of groupthink (Turner & Pratkanis, 1997). In contrast, relationship conflict is negatively associated with such variables (for a revision, see De Dreu & Van Viannen, 2001). In turn, it has been found that relationship conflict affects group climate and reduces team effectiveness (Jehn, 1997).Relationship conflict is defined as an awareness of interpersonal incompatibilities, which includes affective components such as feeling tension and friction. Empirical studies tend to show that relationship, or affective conflict is detrimental to individual and group performance, member satisfaction, and the likelihood the group will work together in the future (Jehn, 1995; Shah & Jehn, 1993). Research findings indicate that the anxiety produced by interpersonal animosity may inhibit cognitive functioning (Roseman, Wiest, & Swartz, 1994; Staw, Sandelands, & Dutton, 1981), as well as distract team members from the task, causing them to work less effectively and produce sub-optimal products (Argyris, 1962; Kelley, 1979).

By contrast, task conflict is an awareness of differences in viewpoints and opinions pertaining to the group's task. It pertains to conflict about ideas and differences of opinion about the task, similar to cognitive conflict (Amason & Sapienza, 1997). Moderate levels of task conflict have been shown to be beneficial to group performance in certain types of tasks (Jehn & Shah, 1997). Task conflict is thought to improve decision quality because the synthesis that emerges from the conflict is generally superior to the individual perspectives themselves (Mason & Mitroff, 1981; Schweiger & Sandberg, 1989; Schwenk, 1990).

These conclusions about the positive function of task conflict and the negative function of relationship conflict, has been based on research that only examined how one type of conflict affects team performance regardless of the other type (e.g. Amason, 1996; Jehn, 1994, 1995). Consistent with this perspective, scholars have tended to recommend management teams to stimulate task conflict and mitigate relationship conflict during team decision making. Nevertheless, the link between task conflict and performance is not perfect. Both kinds of conflict are related. Amason & Mooney (1999) argue that, for some time, researchers have expressed doubt that decision-making could effectively embrace one type of conflict, while simultaneously resisting the other.

Evidence exists that high levels of task conflict can reduce satisfaction and commitment within the team (e.g. Amason & Sapienza, 1997). High levels of task conflict may also cause tension, antagonism, and unhappiness between group members, and an indisposition to work together in the future (Jehn, 1995). Almost all studies, with the exception of Jehn (1995) that measured task and relationship conflict in groups, have shown positive correlations between the two types of conflict (Amason, 1996; De Dreu, 1997; Friedman, Tidd, Currall & Tsai, 2000; Janssen, Van de Vliert & Veenstra, 1999; Jehn, 1995; Jehn & Mannix, 2001; Jehn & Chatman, 2000; Pelled, Eisenhardt & Xin, 1999). A possible explanation for this incongruity is that task-related conflict may turn into relationship conflict (Jehn, 1997). Amason (1996) pointed out that cognitive criticism might easily be interpreted as a personal disapproval or a strategy to enhance one's own position at the expense of someone else's. Baron (1990) showed that a critical evaluation produced negative affective reactions regardless of performance.

Jehn and Chatman (2000), and Janssen, Van de Vliert & Veenstra (1999) view conflict as a complex system of conflict types. In this sense, conflict resolution means that one has to address relative levels of each type of conflict, rather than concentrating on one single type of conflict. Research by Simons and Peterson (2000) provides evidence that task conflict generates relationship conflict. Friedman's study (2000) seems to suggest that the relationship between task conflict and affective variables such as tension at work, are mediated by relationship conflict. However the sign of the relation is not clear; since this effect could work in either direction. For instance, a team member might try to cause difficulties or sabotage the work of a co-worker for personal motives (Jehn, 1995). While it is also possible that certain factors that arouse cognitive conflict might also trigger affective conflict (Amason, 1999).

Recent studies have sometimes identified a third, unique type of conflict, labelled process conflict. It is defined as an awareness of controversies about aspects of how task accomplishment will proceed. More specifically, process conflict pertains to issues of duty and resource delegation such as who should do what or how much one should get. For example, when group members disagree about whose responsibility it is to complete a specific duty, they are experiencing process conflict. Of the three conflict types, process conflict is the least well examined and understood. Indeed, process conflict is not always reliably distinguished from task or relationship conflict (cf. Jehn, 1997; Jehn & Mannix, 2001).

In a small number of cross sectional studies, high levels of process conflict have been negatively related to performance and satisfaction (Jehn, 1997; Jehn, Northcraft, & Neale, 1999; Porter & Lilly, 1996). However, in a recent study of conflict patterns over time, high performing teams were found to have significantly higher levels of process conflict toward the end of the group interaction (but not at the beginning or middle) compared with low performing teams (Jehn & Mannix, 2001). Thus, the findings regarding process conflict are limited, and somewhat contradictory. In addition, the relationship between process conflict and lower levels of performance (at least in some studies) is problematic, especially for leaderless or self-managed teams. In such teams, some level of process conflict seems inevitable. When a team leader is present, typical process decisions made by team managers or leaders are aimed at decreasing conflict over roles and resources (Pondy, 1967), including delegating tasks and responsibilities, setting goals and deadlines, creating schedules, monitoring progress toward goals, dealing with conflicts, and making final decisions on controversial issues (Edelmann, 1993; Pondy, 1967; Wall & Callister, 1995). Because self-managing teams lack a legitimate authority, they must arrive at some agreement about how to handle these procedural matters. As such, they may be prone to repeated or escalating conflicts about process, resulting in potential performance liabilities.

One of the major challenge counted by practicing managers and other stakeholders of contemporary management ethos, is the expressive development of a body of theory to explain why organisational conflicts take the form they do, and why they/others behave as they do, including various stratum of the managerial responses towards conflict dynamics. Outlining some aspects of this emerging line of research on organisations and to call attention to a number of related methodological issues that play an important role in these areas of research – the relation between situational processes, handling strategies and theories, the importance to the research effort of the choice of tautologies and definitions, the nature of evidence, behavioural reengineering, process realignment, organisational preparedness/ adaptability/receptivity and the role of personality-structure interplays among other related domains enshrine the expanding horizons.

Something is *common knowledge* if it is known to each person, and in addition, each person knows that she or he has this knowledge; knows that the other person/s knows the person knows it; and so forth. If in any case, a crevice in this structure entitles a need to acquire the *savoir faire* and to transform the relationship to new heights. It exactly suits for the expanding domains of conflict management studies. Present study is a modest attempt to promote *common knowledge* about conflict management and to share the intricacies of the practice of conflict management with a special emphasise on managerial modes.

3.1 CONFLICT BASICS

Conflict has been defined in many ways depending upon the suitability, focus and group interest. Some conflicts are to be characterised as intrapersonal, while others have been described as interpersonal. Some manifestations of conflict have also been recognised in the organisational context. The common element in most of the past definitions of conflict includes-

- Conflict involves opposing interests between parties in a zero sum or negative-sum situation (whatever one player wins, the other loses so that the total benefit of the two players is zero-hence the name. (Micheal Nicholson, 1970)).
- The parties must be aware of the opposing interests between them.
- Each party must believe that the other will thwart or has already thwarted her or his interests.

- ✪ Conflict is a process arising from past and current interactions and the context in which they took place.

- ✪ There seems to be a hidden message that conflict process can bring changes and a positive frame if applied appropriately.

- ✪ Although conflict is normally applied in interpersonal context, conflict process can be initiated and sustained by an individual, interpersonal level, group level or at a system level.

3.2 CHANGING VIEWS OF CONFLICT

Over the years, three distinct philosophies that refer to different managerial attitudes toward conflicts have been identified- the classical, behavioural and the modern interactionist philosophies. The classical approach viewed conflicts as an organisational abnormality, a potentially dangerous process. By this conflict induces mainly negative aspects- anger, resentment, confusion, lack of cooperation, etc. It was regarded as disrupting the smooth functioning of organisational processes and creates chaos and disorder. Conflict is 'bad' and must be avoided at all costs. The organisational structure with its clear policies, elaborated rules and well defined specifications of authority and responsibility should not permit conflicts. Conflicts will not occur if sound management principles are applied. By any chance if conflicts were to develop, the management can easily and quickly resolves them.

Managerial attitude towards conflict was one of fear and disdain. Conflict, by definition was viewed as harmful and was to be avoided as per this philosophy. Behaviouralists also had a similar jaundiced view of conflict. They also believed that conflict, by definition was harmful and should be avoided. Those who generated conflict were troublemakers and were bad for the organisation. This view reflected a "popular preoccupation with morals, human relations and cooperation and the general value that peace is good and conflict bad" (Robbins, 1991). They however accepted the fact that conflict is a natural occurrence in all organisations.

The emerging view of conflict, called as interactionist view, reverses many of the cozy nostrums of human relations management. The interactionist view recognises that the conflict occurs as a process or sequence of events. These events take place in conflict episodes between the parties. Whenever the interactions happen, there exist a wider scope for conflict and its management of the same in organisational context was highly appreciated by this perspective.

The process of conflict does not occur in a vacuum. Rather they are shaped by structural parameters of the system, the relatively fixed or slow changing conditions influencing events at the interface between the parties. It recognises that in some cases conflict may be helpful, facilitative and functional. Thus, conflict management traveled its journey through avoidance, acceptance and encouragement and stimulation. The current thought acknowledges the inevitability of conflict and focuses it as a useful tool / vehicle to shake the organisation from stereo type / contention to innovation and creativity.

3.3 ORGANISATIONAL CONFLICT IN MODERN PERSPECTIVE- INTEGRATIVE VIEW

- Conflict is not an organisational abnormality. On the other hand, it is a normal aspect of organisational intercourse. It is a fact of industrial life that must understood rather that fought.
- Conflict is inevitable, sometimes desirable. It is an inherent structural component in the organisational relations.
- Conflict is neither bad nor good for organisations. Perfect organisational health is not free from conflicts.
- Troublemakers do not always cause conflict. It is rather determined by structural factors like the design of a career structure, the physical shape of a building, etc.
- Conflict is integral to the nature of change.

3.4 WAVES OF STYLE AND AMOUNT OF CONFLICT

Studies on the management of organisational conflict have taken two directions. Some researchers have attempted to measure the amount of conflict at various organisational levels and to explore the sources of such conflict. Implicit in these studies is that a moderate amount of conflict may be maintained for increasing organisational effectiveness by altering the sources of conflict. Others had attempted to relate the various styles of handling interpersonal conflict of the organisational participants and their effects on quality of problem solution or attainment of social system objectives. It becomes evident that the distinction between the 'amount of conflict' at various levels and the styles of handling interpersonal conflict is essential for a proper understanding of the nature of conflict management. In recent years, some researchers have used the indices of tension, annoyance, disputes, distrust, disagreement, etc to measure the amount of conflict at various levels. These are measures of the amount of conflict which are quite distinct from the styles of handling conflict (Rahim, 1992).

There are two basic approaches to intervention in conflict- behavioural and structural (Rahim, 1977; Rahim & Bonoma, 1979). The behavioural approach attempts to improve organisational effectiveness by changing members' culture- attitudes, values, norms, beliefs, etc. The behavioural approach is mainly designed to manage conflict by enabling the organisational participants to learn the various styles of handling interpersonal conflict and the situations where they are appropriate. The technique of role analysis may be used to enable organisational members to deal with their intrapersonal conflict functionally. Other behavioural science techniques, such as transactional analysis, team building, and intergroup problem solving may be used to enable the organisational members to deal with interpersonal, intragroup, and intergroup conflicts, respectively.

The structural approach attempts to improve organisational effectiveness by changing the organisation's structural design characteristics– differentiation and integration mechanisms, system of communication, reward structure, etc. This approach mainly attempts to manage conflict by altering the amount of conflict experienced by the organisational members at various levels. The structural interventions, such as job design, provision for ombudsman, analysis of group tasks, and analysis of task interdependence of two or more groups may be used to reduce or generate conflict at intrapersonal, interpersonal, intragroup, and intergroup conflicts, respectively.

3.6 INTERACTIONIST APPROACH

Likert and Likert have extended the concept of participatory management to the areas of conflict management, and have given enough evidence to show that a more participatory style of management improves conflict management. Blake, Shepard and Mouton have suggested different approaches and styles of conflict management. They have proposed that three basic assumptions or orientations are important in relation to conflict management – (a) conflicts are inevitable and agreement is impossible ; (b) conflicts are not inevitable, and yet agreement is not possible; and (c) although there is conflict, agreement is possible. They suggest that these three orientations get combined with three degrees of active-passive attitude (active orientation having high stakes, and passive orientation having low stakes). A combination of three assumption about conflict and three orientations of activeness give nine different modes of conflict handling, they call it as modes of conflict resolution.

Content-dominant theories highlight the different aspects of conflict managerial concepts whereas, process-dominant theories refine the cognizant, preferred or imposed choice process of conflict process dynamics. Content-dominant theory only guarantees that the elemental domination of content is very much there and it does not exclude the process or other element although in varying degrees. The above factor is equally applicable to the process-dominant theories as well.

3.9 CONTENT-DOMINANT THEORIES

Major content-dominant theories include the various approach theories of organisational conflict management, realistic conflict theories, relative deprivation theory, and psycho cultural theory besides the inclusion of components of universalistic notations as well as that of normative or contingency approaches.

3.9.1 Organisational approach theories

In his review of the past and present trends in the field of conflict theory and research, Beaumont (1996) distinguished the organisation theory approach to conflict from the industrial relations approach and emphasised the importance of negotiation and networking in non union contexts. He considered the differing perspectives with each. With respect to organisation theory, he argued that before the 1960s, mainstream organisation theory essentially ignored conflict. Classics works such as those of Henri Fayol did not discuss it at all and treated organisations as apolitical systems.

The earliest references to conflict are to be found in the work of Louis Pondy (1967). Although he failed to integrate the topic into mainstream organisation theory, Pondy did make two substantiate points. First, conflict could be naturally occurring phenomenon, that is it was endemic to organisations and second, that it was not necessarily a bad thing. Pondy wrote in the 1960s which were also the high-water mark of contingency theory. The main message of his theory was that there was no one best way to manage the conflicts. This theory focused on fitting one's strategy to one's particular environment and circumstances. Contingency theory did not talk about conflict. It is only fairly recently that main-stream organisation theory has really begun to discuss conflict in an analytical way. The work of Jeffrey Pieffer (1981) was important because it stressed intra-managerial conflict. This is the perspective that holds that an organisation is , in essence a loose grouping of sectional coalition forces that there is a great deal of variance in sub unit power within organisations and that decisions have to be negotiated and bargained over.

Martin (1992) distinguished the differentiative and fragmentative perspectives to the subject as standing alongside the currently popular integrationist-unitary one. In order to explain the nature of negotiation and conflict, Pieffer and his colleagues drew heavily on Emerson's (1962) perspective of power dependency. That is, A has power over B because he has control of resources that B cannot obtain from elsewhere.

Pieffer's and Martin's approaches represent a significant move away from the rational, decision making paradigm of organisations and emphasise the importance of the political model of organisations. Alongside the traditional organisational theories, which has moved from the apolitical, rationalist perspective to the sectional conflict-negotiating perspective another perspective has been discerned. This is the unitarist perspective which originated in the 1930s with Elton Mayo and the human relation school of thought. The linear development of that school of research and writing was the organisational change and development literature of the 1960s. The most recent stage of this unitarist school of thinking is represented by William Ouchi's (1981) Theory Z and the work of Peters and Waterman (1982) and their successors. These authors differ from the mainstream organisational theorists mentioned earlier in that, while they recognise conflict, they regard it as neither legitimate nor desirable. Moreover, they propose that it can be solved through increased trust and open communications. Whilst this perspective on conflict is limited, it does nevertheless recognise that conflict exists. These writers advocate an integrationist perspective on corporate culture, recommending that culture should reflect the values of senior management and be embodied in a company value statement. The human resources policy mix within the firm should be designed so as to encourage employees to have these corporate culture values incorporated. The assumption made is that high culture organisations are also high performance organisations partly at least through being conflict free.

The second body of knowledge to be considered in relation to conflict theory is industrial relations. This literature has conflict at its core. There are two perspectives within it. The first is the Marxist perspective which sees conflict as emanating from outside the organisation. It derives from wider ownership control structures within society at large. The second and more mainstream industrial relations literature derives from the pluralist tradition which sees conflict as inevitable and to some extent desirable within an organisation. Such inevitability is the result of the differences in interest between management and workers. Management is committed to change as it relates to dynamic organisational performance. The workers in contrast are more status quo- oriented requiring job security.

The pluralist perspective also makes the point that conflict arises from the superior-subordinate relationship. Once there is a hierarchy, some degree of conflict is inevitable and arguable desirable. A good pluralist will qualify that statement by saying that the conflict, in order to produce positive advantages must be functional in nature. However a pluralist cannot operationalise the notion of functional conflict. There is no empirical way of saying when the conflict is too high or too low. A pluralist talk instead about the need for institutional channels to ensure that conflict does not take an unacceptably destructive form. They traditionally look to collective bargaining and trade unionism to institutionalise and functionalise conflict.

Within the industrial relations paradigm, the pluralists differ from someone like Pieffer in trying to operationalise the determinants of conflict. Pieffer's approach goes back to the sociological perspective of Emerson's power dependency notion of control over resources and the ability to minimise organisational uncertainty. The industrial relations paradigm in contrast draws heavily on Neil Chamberlain's (1951) work, which stresses not so much intra management conflict as employee- management- union conflict. There, the emphasis is on trying to operationalise the notion of bargaining power where the perspective is on the costs of agreement relative to the costs of disagreement. Thus the union or the bargaining group will have increased power in relation to management if it can increase the costs of management disagreeing with the union's demand or lower the costs of management agreeing to the union's demand.

Beamount (1996) argued that developments such as the organisation of the future, globalisation, networking and flatter hierarchy were likely to enhance the importance of both negotiation and conflict resolution practices. This was because the more equally that power was distributed in an organisation; the more likely it was that conflicts of interests and goals would surface as open conflicts. In a sense, organisations were becoming more political. In addition, conflict was likely to become more complex in nature, as negotiation come to involve more parties and not just the union and management with their clearly defined and fixed identities.

These developments have a number of implications. First, an increase of networking by the firms, that is the use of strategic alliances across national boundaries has led to an interest in cross cultural negotiations and conflict resolution practices like that of strategic joint ventures.

Weiss (1994) argued that given the diversity of interests in modern organisations, there was a need for flexible, multi-option avenues for resolving differences before they escalated into costly win-lose or lose-lose situations. Second, the increase in the number of non union associations and costs of legal cases has led to the emergence of Alternative Dispute Resolution systems in their organisations.

Alternative Dispute Resolution systems emphasise managerial practices to eliminate the root causes of problems, the use of informal participatory processes to encourage the resolving of problems close to their source and the use of trained mentors, peers, facilitators and ombudsmen to replace expensive outside legal settlements (Rowe, 1993). It is not surprising that the renewed interest in the alternative approaches expanded its horizons by the great industrial management stalwarts like Fisher (1981, 1992), Weiss (1993) among others. All have a strong emphasis on win–win bargaining as opposed to the traditional adversarial approach in their recommendations.

3.9.2 Realistic Conflict Theories

Realistic conflict theory views conflict between groups as generated by an interdependent competition for scarce resources (Bobo, 1983; Hogg & Abrams, 1988). The zero-sum competitive relationship (i.e., only one group can attain a desired goal) between the in-group and out-group is considered to be the source of conflict. The outcome of a zero-sum competition necessarily dictates that one group be higher in status than the other. The possibility of not obtaining the scarce resource thus indicates that the perceived status and value of the in-group is threatened. In an effort to retain value in the face of conflict, a threat to the value of group membership should lead to behaviours that assist the in-group in obtaining the resource. In support of this idea, the presence of realistic conflict has been found to elicit both in-group favouritism and out-group derogation. For example, in-group favouritism was found in laboratory conditions where an interdependent goal was present, compared to a condition where no goal was present (Scheepers, Spears, Doosje, & Manstead, 2002).

Brown, Condor, Mathews, Wade, and Williams (1986) found that perceived realistic conflict predicted employees' intergroup differentiation (the perception of greater differences between the in-group and a relevant out-group), a precursor to in-group favouritism. When explored in racial and ethnic group settings, realistic conflict has been found to predict prejudice towards immigrants (Bizman & Yinon, 2001; Zárate, Garcia, Garza, & Hitlan,

2004).As group members focus on the attempts to retain value by increasing in-group favouritism and out-group derogation, they will be accordingly less likely to perform behaviours that appear to help rather than hinder the out-group in the conflict. In-group members who perceive the out-group to be in competition for scarce resources are unlikely to directly aid the other group in attaining the resource.

3.9.3 Relative Deprivation Theory

Relative deprivation theory considers conflict to arise from perceptions of unequal and unfairly discrepant outcomes between groups. The group-based form of relative deprivation, fraternal relative deprivation, is based on social comparisons between one's own and other groups where one's in-group is disadvantaged by a perceived outcome inequality. Group members believe that their group deserves an outcome, and if they do not receive the outcome yet observe a referent other group unfairly receiving that outcome, they experience relative deprivation (Ellemers, 2002; Hogg & Abrams, 1988). Relative deprivation is dependent upon an outcome with two essential properties- inequality and injustice (or illegitimacy). Tyler and Blader (2003) argue that justice is central to how people construct their social identities, as justice helps maintain a secure and positive identity. Therefore, if an unjust group outcome or process is perceived, it is likely that the previously-secure identity with the group is threatened. Fraternal relative deprivation differs from the individually-based egoistic deprivation, which arises from a comparison between the self and others, not between groups. Fraternal relative deprivation has been studied as a precursor to social collective action (Wright & Tropp, 2002), especially among disadvantaged groups in society (e.g., Tougas & Veilleux, 1988). Low-status group members whose status was due to illegitimate treatment were found to discriminate more in   of the in-group when their disadvantage was seen to be less legitimate (Ellemers, Wilke, & Van Knippenberg, 1993). Resentment on behalf of the group (relative deprivation) was found to mediate the relationship between identification with a group and in-group favouritism (Mummendey, Kessler, Klink, & Mielke, 1999). Theoretical development by Wright and Tropp (2002) posits that when in-group status is illegitimate (indicating the presence of relative deprivation), groups and individuals will engage in action inconsistent with social rules.

3.9.4 Psycho cultural conflict theory

According to Marc Howard Ross (1993), a psycho cultural analysis is based on the understanding that much social action is ambiguous; this approach stresses the importance of the interpretation of words and deeds in explaining why some disputes unleash intense and violent sequences and why others do not. Thus, it is relevant to the intensity of conflicts. Contemporary psychoanalytic ideas are particularly helpful in thinking about the psycho cultural construction of social worlds (Greenberg and Mitchell 1983; Stern 1985; Volkan 1988). Those works emphasised social communication and interaction from the first days of life, placing psychological development squarely in the social realm.

Psycho cultural approach draws our attention to how early relationships create a model, or template, for later ones and provide a set of standards by which groups and individuals evaluate their social worlds. Ross (1989) further states that what individuals share is emphasised both affectively and cognitively, whereas deviations from the norm are selectively ignored or negatively reinforced as incompatible with group membership. He continues by saying that dispositions learned early in life are not only relevant on the perceptual level; they are also implicated in specific behavioural patterns which serve one throughout life, such as how to respond to perceived insults, when to use physical aggression, or whom to trust. The translation of dispositional tendencies into behavioural patterns occurs on the individual level but is fundamentally a social process; where there is social support for certain types of actions they will be learned and maintained; where they are disapproved of they become less common.

3.9.5 Universalistic theories

Universalistic theories have often been referred to as normative within the conflict literature, because they specify a single correct way of doing things and thus internalised, can lead to the formation of a norm (Lewicki, 1985; Thomas, 1982). However, the word normative is often used elsewhere simply as a synonym for prescriptive. Obviously, contingency theories and universalistic theories can be used prescriptively. In conflict literature, the word normative is used in the more restrictive sense, pertaining to norms and norm- related reasoning.

Thus Content-dominated theories may seems to focus on what makes conflict management and try to explain the facets of the constituents of management essentials for handling the conflicts at various levels.

3.10 PROCESS DOMINATED THEORIES

Process-dominant theories include the threshold theory of conflict, attribution theories, arousal and aggression theories, group coalition extension theory, extended group faultline theory, consensus and the struggle for control theory and Distraction-Conflict theories among others.

3.10.1 The threshold theory of conflict

According to Ernest Bormann, groups experience two types of social tension-primary and secondary. Primary tension occurs during the orientation phase when group members feel too restrained by the novelty of the group setting. Secondary tension usually occurs when group's routine patterns of interaction are disrupted by intense disagreement. Although Bormann admits that uncontrolled secondary conflict can destroy the group, he argues that every group has a threshold for tension that represents its optimal level of conflict among the members. Thereby the emphasis was clearly on the positive value of the conflict. Conflict, too below the optimal level; results in group apathy, boredom and lack of involvement. Prolonged conflict above the optimal level on the other hand causes shared disagreement, heightened hostility and a loss of group effectiveness. What is needed then is a balance between too little tension and too much tension. In an ideal situation, group experiences frequent episodes of conflict, these episodes have mostly positive consequences- the clarification of goals, an increased understanding of differences and points of contention, successful discussion, stimulation of interests and the release of hostility. The lively interactions enable a group to apparently manage and develop techniques that limit escalation and thereby to control the magnitude and longevity of the conflict (Tuckman, 1965; Bormann, 1975).

3.10.2 Attribution theories

According to attribution theory, which is a social psychological explanation of how people continually formulate intuitive causes of behaviours and events that transpire in the organisational set up or in the groups(Heider, 1958). During conflict, interactants make attributions about their associates' motives and intentions, and these inferences steer their interpretation of the situation. When group members argue, for example they must determine why they disagree. If members conclude that their disagreement stems merely from the group's attempts to make the right decision, the disagreement will probably not turn into true conflict. However if participants attribute the disagreement to others' incompetence, belligeance or argumentativeness- a simple disagreement can escalate into an impetuous conflict (Horai, 1977).

If the conflicting parties' attributions were always accurate, they would help interactants understand one another better and thereby function as conflict managers. Unfortunately perceptual biases regularly distort individuals' attributional inferences. One bias occurs when attributors assume that other peoples' behaviour is caused by dispositional rather than situational factors. The fundamental attribution error will point out the ill conceived notations against the other persons' personality, beliefs, attitudes, and values for the conflict to rise to alarming levels (Kelley, 1979). The distortion would be minimal when the interpersonal interactions are pleasant or interactants are careful to empathise with one another, but the effect grows stronger during conflict (Regan &Totten, 1975).

Researchers in a series of studies compared the attributions of active observers, those who not only observed others but also interacted with the others – to the attributions of passive observers, individuals who were not actually part of the group. When these two sets of observers later estimated the extent to which the behaviour of the partner was a good indicator of personality, active observers made more dispositional attributions than passive observers, provided the other party had competed. In other words the bias was greatest during conflict situations (Miller & Norman, 1975; Murata, 1982).

These findings and others suggest that people had a tendency to assume the worst about the other members in their organisations. In one study subjects played like that of a Prisoner's Dilemma Game with another whose behaviour was ranging from Competitive to altruistic. When asked to describe their partner's motives, participants were most accurate in interpreting cooperation and altruism. Apparently, the members had difficulty believing that their associates were behaving in an altruistic manner but readily believed the suggestion that their behaviours revealed conflict (Maki, Thorngate, 1979; Prunnet, 1998).

Similarly, Harold Kelley et al (1970, 1989) found that people who tend to compete with others are less accurate in their perceptions than individuals who tend to cooperate. When cooperators play with the other cooperators, their perceptions of their partner's strategy are inaccurate only less than 6% of the time. When competitors play with the cooperators, however they misinterpret their partner's strategy more than 47% of the time, mistakenly believing that the cooperators are competing.

3.10.3 Arousal and aggression Theories

As conflict escalates, anxiety and tension become more dominant (Blascovich, Nash, & Ginsburg, 1978; Van Egeren, 1979). Even when group members begin by discussing their points calmly and dispassionately, as they become locked into their positions; emotional expressions begin to replace logical discussions. Unfortunately, this emotional arousal often exacerbates the conflict. Evidence of this conflict-stimulating effect of emotional arousal comes from the studies of the arousal /aggression hypothesis. This hypothesis is based on early studies of the link between frustration and aggression (Berkowitz, 1989). When group members are unable to attain the goals they desire because of some environmental restraint or personal limitation, they sometimes experience frustration. This frustration, in turn, produces a readiness to respond in an aggressive manner that boils over into hostility if situational cues that serve as releasers are present. Recent research indicates that many unpleasant and noxious conditions, including competition, insults, failures and stress can set the stage for aggressive conflict. These aversive events work by creating a heightened emotional arousal, which is often subjectively labeled anger. This arousal then is the motivation driving the subsequent aggressive actions (Zilmann, 1983, 1996).

John French in an early laboratory study of conflict in groups (1941) demonstrated the link between arousal and aggression by examining the reactions of various groups as they worked on a series of insoluble problems. In groups composed of subjects who had never interacted before the meeting, frustration led to deep divisions in the group. In a similar study Berkowitz et al (1998) found systematic differences among the group members. When the group members knew one another before the actual interaction, the frustration did not produce as much separation between members but interpersonal aggression such as overt hostility, scapegoating and domination was relatively high.

3.10.4 Group coalition extension theory

In many instances conflict in a group occurs because members must compete for the limited organisational resources. Deutsch, a leading researcher in the area, notes that such competition creates contrient interdependence among the group members, whereas cooperation leads to promotive interdependence. Mixed- motive situations, like the prisoner's dilemma and social traps stimulate conflict because they tempt individuals to compete rather than cooperate. Once individuals begin to compete in each situation, cooperation is difficult to establish.

The use of contentious influence strategies, such as threats and punishments also tends to heighten the conflicts, particularly if all the parties in the confrontation have the capacity to threaten one another. Though the relationship between the personal characteristics of members and group behaviour is complicated, people who adopt a competitive interpersonal mode tend to generate more conflict than cooperators. The conflict when becomes visible and felt often intensifies before it begins abate. This conflict spiral is produced by a host of factors, including misperceptions, commitment, entrapment, arousal, reciprocity and coalitions. The attribution theory suggests that conflict is exacerbated by the parties' tendencies to misperceive others and to assume that the other parties' behaviour is caused by personal (dispositional) rather than situational (environmental) factors. This fundamental attribution error is particularly strong during conflict, with the result that people tend to assume the worst about other members.

When individuals defend their viewpoints in groups, attitude elaboration, the need to save face, rationalisation and reactance can all combine to increase their commitment to their position. If this commitment becomes over commitment, entrapment can occur. Further conflict is often arousing. The arousal/ aggression hypothesis predicts that group members will be ready to respond in an aggressive manner. The norm of reciprocity by sanctioning the matching of competition with the competition is partly responsible for the behavioural assimilation seen when a cooperative individual must work with a competitive one.

Although conflict may be confined during the initial stages; when coalition forms, the rest of the group is often drawn into the fracas. Coalitions represent a unique form of intragroup conflict. Forming coalition in most cases a contentious influence strategy that increases competition rather than cooperation among the members of coalition. Through the use of simulation experiments in which subjects form coalitions in order to win points, researchers have found that coalitions tend to include only the minimum number of members necessary exercising the option of cheapest winning solution, be small rather than large, include relatively weak members, exclude powerful new entrants, and differ depending on the issues of gender, race, language, etc. Bargaining theory seems to offer a better explanation of coalition process than either minimum resource theory or minimum power theory the distribution of resources gained through the joint venture be it a real or imaginary because of the coalition formation is often determined by bargaining, concessions, objections, threats and other active interventions from the members.

3.10.5 Extended group faultline theory

Using the coalition theory (Caplow, 1956; Komorita & Kravitz, 1983; Mack & Snyder, 1957; Murnighan,1978) and Schneider's attraction-selection-attrition model of organisational membership (1983), Davidson et al (1991) expanded group faultline theory and propose that if more demographic attributes align in the same way (faultline strength), group members in each subgroup will perceive the similarity within their subgroup. Since similar members are likely to interact with each other more often and find their interactions pleasant and more desirable, they will be likely to form coalitions (Byrne, 1971; Pool, 1976; Roger & Bhowmik, 1971; Stevenson, Pearce, & Porter, 1985). Due to the similarity among group members involved in coalition formation, the conflict within subgroups is apt to decline. However, the existence of coalitions is likely to amplify the salience of in-group/out-group membership causing strain and polarisation between subgroups (Hogg, Turner, & Davidson, 1990).

Once coalitions are formed, the negative effects of stereotyping, in-group favouritism and out-group hostility are likely to sharpen the boundary salience around coalitions and strengthen conflict between them. These group processes are likely to lead to intensification of conflict between subgroups and therefore, promote or activate intergroup conflict. In particular three types of conflict that have been identified in working groups, bicultural teams, and organising entities (Amason, 1996; Jehn, 1997; Jehn and Jageuri, 2001; Jehn, Northcraft, and Neale, 1999; Pelled, 1996; Shah and Jehn, 1993)as well as of inter-subgroup relationships in groups(Hogg et.al 1990) were key constituents of this theory.

3.10.6 Consensus and the struggle for control theory

Conflicts of interest can arise in teams through deliberate design. When team members have to propose as well implement projects, conflicts can reduce cooperation at the implementation stage, and lower incentives to take high effort towards conceiving a strategy. At the same time, since any member desires control at the execution stage only when there are conflicts of interest, increased conflicts can raise the competition for control through creation of superior policy. This trade-off determines whether the principal can gain from the presence of such 'beneficial conflict'. These kinds of conflicts can also be used to understand teamwork, and indeed, fractious teams may prove to be superior platforms for resolving free-rider problems when compared to individual or segregated production. Further, the principal's incentive to choose disputatious teams may be greater when team size is larger.

This theory proposes a perspective on conflict that differs, through its stress on the relation with consensus and the struggle for control, from existing functional theories (see, e.g., Coser,1956 and Simmel,1968), which typically focus on the role of conflict as an 'integrative force' (Simmel , 1955) in society. The results may be useful in comprehending some of the tensions between competition and cooperation in various team or community settings, and the role such strains play in modulating incentive problems. In the context of leadership, the analysis can help understand whether a principal should select a team whose members have well-aligned interests and therefore adopt a cooperative or consensual style of operation, or whether he should encourage 'creative tension' between them. It may also be interesting to investigate the impact of control allocation on the resolution of incentive problems in more general settings, and whether conflicts between vested competitors' influence the distribution of authority-this and many other interrelated factors are conveniently put aside for future enhancers of this theory.

Positional heterogeneity amongst team members is a common feature in many organisations. Members, even while jointly pursuing the common goal of team success, may have differing biases, opinions, interests, divisional objectives, departmental prerogatives, etc. These differences can lead to a diminution of consensus and an exacerbation of conflicts of interest, which can make teamwork difficult and lead to lower team performance. The problem of team conflict has long been recognised in studies of organisational behaviour and structure, and managerial and political leadership (see, e.g., Drucker (1974), George (1980) and Priem (1990)). Team leaders have often been criticised for permitting excessive conflicts, and been commended for adopting a more consensual approach (see, e.g., Katzenbach and Smith (1993), Kakabadse and Smyllie (1994) and Hambrick (1995)). At the same time, it has also been recognised that there may be benefits to encouraging 'productive conflict' (Brown, 1983) or 'constructive conflict' (De Janasz, Dowd and Schneider, 2001) in teams. Conflict in a group can take many forms. Disagreements that arise when one person misinterprets another's position or actions are termed false conflicts (Deutsch, 1973) or autistic conflicts (Holmes & Miller, 1976; Kriesberg, 1973). Other conflicts, sometimes called contingent conflicts, are easily solved by changing some minor situational factors. The group member who arouses the ire of others by consistently arriving for meetings ten minute late can be told to show up on time or be dropped from the group; the discord over who sits where at the rectangular table may be alleviated by moving to a round table. Such disagreements, although of some importance to the group, are easily manageable without any undue increase in group tension (Deutsch, 1973).

Escalating conflict, in contrast, can seriously disrupt the group's internal dynamics. Even when the conflict stems from a minor point of disagreement, such as how to control the flow of communication or when to break for lunch, it can lead to other, more basic points of contentiousness. More issues are brought out into the open, and soon the minor differences extent to many areas. Further members who were reluctant to break the smooth pre conflict interaction now realise that the damage is already done and they join in the fray by expressing the dislikes and disagreements that they had previously suppressed. In spite of the decelerating connotations of the conflict, disagreeing is a natural consequence of joining a group. Observers of all types of groups have documented clashes among the members and have invariably concluded that group conflict is as common as group harmony (Benn's & Shepard, 1956; Fisher, 1980; Tuckman, 1965). The dynamic nature of the group ensures continual change, but along with the change comes stresses and strains that surface in the form of conflict because their actions are perfectly coordinated, but in most groups the push and pull of interpersonal forces inevitably exerts its influence (Dahrendorf, 1958, 1959). Lewis Coser goes as far as to suggest that although conflicts can destroy a group, it can also promote group unity. The idea that conflict creates unification may seem paradoxical, but Coser observed that conflict which serve to sew the social system together by cancelling each other out, thus prevent disintegration along one primary line of cleavage (1956, p.80).

Eminent thinkers on the group philosophy have noted that interdependency among the members and the stability of a group cannot deepen until hostility has surfaced, been confronted, and been resolved (Benn &Shepard, 1956; Deutsch, 1973). Low levels of conflict in a group could be an indication of remarkably positive interpersonal relations, but it is more likely that the group members are simply uninvolved, demotivated and bored. Coser notes that the absence of conflict tells us little about the stability of the group since the more cohesive the group, the more intense is the conflict. Conflict also provides a means of venting personal hostilities but members can reduce this stress by confronting the problem and communicating dissatisfactions honestly and openly. If hostilities are never expresses in the group, they may build up to a point at which the group can no longer continue as a unit and the functioning of the group would be at its stake (Tuckman, 1965).

3.10.7 Line- staff conflict theories

In his classic study, Melville Dalton studied the conflict between line managers, those directly responsible for production, and staff managers, those not directly involved but performing an advisory or staff functions. Line managers are afraid that staff specialists will intrude on their jobs and reduce their authority and power, staff specialists complain that line managers do not make good use of them or provide them with enough authority. Dalton also found that conflict could result because staff specialists consider their knowledge is superior and up to date when compared with the line managers. Whereas the line managers had a hunch that they have the real time exposure and that brings them the real capacity to take pragmatic decisions.

Further staff member's loyalty to the company was also questioned by the line managers as they are relatively new entrants to the organisation and are alien to the customary practices that are essentially basic for their organisation. Loyalty to the discipline rather than to the organisation was also raised by the line managers against the staff specialists. On the other hand the closed mind set of the line managers were questioned by the staff specialists and thus creating every room for an active conflicting interactions within the organisation.

3.10.8 System component conflict theories

Various components in the organisation with its set of policies, procedures and the workflow mechanism are prone to conflicts in a way or other. The functional smooth inflow and organisational workings are often highly depends upon a group of factors or organisational system elements. The interrelatedness among the factors often brings friction and creates the need to reintroduce or creatively redistribute the organisational energy to more positive phases of action.

Formal conflicts within organisation arise when employees do not follow formal procedures and communication channels (Jameson, 1999). Sources of conflict may refer to different ideas, opinions, attitudes (Jehn, 1995; 1997). Managers representing various departments develop attitudes based on different cultures and beliefs (Deshpande & Webster, 1993). On another issue the fact that certain departments gather non formal power leads to high conflict intensity within organisation (Ruekert & Walker, 1987). One department that has negotiating power tries to dominate decisions using non formal power (Lawrence & Lorsch, 1967). Effectiveness of collaboration between departments is influenced by the perception of how much this collaboration is productive and satisfying for different parties (Ruekert & Walker, 1987).

When information flow and joint decision- making is underdeveloped (Kahn, 1996) while managers develop stereotypes each other lacking appreciation and trust (Souder, 1981). Cooperation between managers from different departments (sales, production, R&D, marketing) within cross- functional teams is a critical factor for success. On general joint decision making and information sharing is necessary in order to achieve competitive advantage and meet customer needs (Weinrauch & Anderson 1982). The development of participative management contributes effectively into the integration of procedures and processes (Shaw & Shaw, 1998). Under the above condition managers from different functions integrate their cultures in a higher degree, decreasing intensity of conflict and developing emotions of trust.

3.10.9 Distraction-Conflict theories

Distraction-conflict theories assume that audiences and coactors in conflictual situations increase the parties' arousal and influence in many ways their behaviour (Baron, 1986; Sanders, 1983). In contrast to earlier views, however, distraction- conflict theories suggests that such arousal stems from conflict between two tendencies- (a) the tendency to pay attention to the task being performed, and (b) the tendency to direct attention to an audience or coactors. Such conflict is arousing, and such arousal, in turn, enhances the tendency to perform dominant responses. If these are correct in a given situation, performance is enhanced; if they are incorrect, performance is impaired. While *distraction-conflict theories* may not provide a final answer to the persistent puzzle of psychosocial facilitation, it has certainly added substantially to our understanding of those processes including drive-responses, public-private behaviour, individualistic-participative behaviour and most importantly individuals' belongingness to a team/group/organisation.

3.11 CONFLICT MANAGEMENT MODELS

There exists a plethora of conflict management models. Some of them are directly addressing the conflict and others in circuitous ways. It seems that dual perceptive-explanatory models are popularly followed and widely appreciated by many practitioners and academicians. Individual as a member of the group, in an organisational context is the most addressed managerially acclaimed mechanism for determining the conflict handling strategies/styles explained through many of the models.

3.11.1 Group Identification Model

Inspection of conflict management patterns along this model was based on integration of two widely used models- the Dual Concern Model (Blake & Mouton, 1964; Pruitt & Rubin, 1986; Rahim, 1983) and the *Exit, Voice, Loyalty, Neglect Model* (EVLN Model, Rusbult, 1993), portraying individual reactions to dissatisfaction in relationships. The integrated model comprises five possible patterns of conflict management- Dominance (active-destructive), integration (active-constructive), compromising (active-constructive), obliging (passive-constructive) and avoidance (passive-destructive).The dual concern model, based on motivational dimensions - concern for self and concern for the other - contributed the situational/motivational variable, namely group identification. From the EVLN model concerning with reactions to relationship dissatisfaction, dispositional variable of global and social self-efficacy were drawn to this model by past researchers.

Group identification refers to the perceived relationship of the individual members with the specific group to which he or she belongs. It taps three dimensions- the cognitive that is the member's perception of the group as an element of the self; the affective dimension, namely attraction and positive feelings towards the group; and behavioural dimension encompassing perceived interdependence among the group members required to attain the group goals (Henry, Arrow, & Carini, 1999).

Research has indicated that a person with a higher sense of identification with the group was more likely to select cooperative alternatives, that is cooperate with other group members in contrast with individuals with lower sense of group identification (De-Cremer, 2001). In a similar vein, Rusbult (1993) found that individuals who felt highly committed to their relationships tended to exhibit constructive responses to crisis in interpersonal relationship. Consequently, it was assumed that group identification would be associated with a cooperative motivation, namely a desire to seek constructive ways to deal with intra-group conflict. Obviously the level of identification with the group constitutes a situational variable; it is determined by the particular group to which the individual belongs and her or his perceptions of that collective unit. In addition to learning about the relationship between a factor and conflict management patterns, past researchers were interested to examine the association of dispositional variables to group members' coping modes with intra-group conflict, notably the individuals' self-perceptions of social efficacy.

3.11.2 Multiple sources model

Multiple sources model of conflict proposes three fundamental causes of conflict in organisations-identity-related differences, role incompatibility, and environmental stress.

Identity-related differences- Individuals bring different personal backgrounds, experiences, and cultural values when they enter organisations thus creating their own individual and unique identities. Different socialisation processes, levels of education, and so forth, shape their experiences and values. As a result, their interpretations of events and their expectations about relationships with others in the organisation will vary considerably. Conflicts caused by incongruent personal values *that stem from* these social identities are among the most difficult to resolve because they evoke values we hold deeply.

Role Incompatibility- The complexity inherent in most organisations tends to produce conflict between members whose tasks are interdependent but whose roles are incompatible. This type of conflict is exemplified by the ubiquitous goal conflicts between line and staff, production and sales, marketing, and R and D. Each unit has different responsibilities in the organisation, and as a result each places different priorities on organisational goals (e.g., customer satisfaction, product quality, production efficiency, and compliance with government regulations). It is also typical of firms whose multiple product lines compete for scarce resources. Role incompatibility conflicts may overlap with those arising from identity differences. The personal differences among the members bring to an organisation generally remain dormant until they are triggered by an organisational catalyst, like interdependent task responsibilities. And one reason members often perceive that their assigned roles are incompatible is that they are operating from different bases of information. They communicate with different sets of people, are tied into different reporting systems, and receive instructions from different bosses.

Environmental Stress- Another major source of conflict is environmentally induced stress. Conflicts stemming from identity differences and role incompatibilities are greatly exacerbated by a stressful environment. Uncertainty in the environment also fosters conflict. When individuals find it difficult to predict what is going to happen to them from month to month, they become very anxious and prone to conflict. This type of 'frustration conflict' often stems from rapid, repeated change. If task assignments, management philosophy, accounting procedures, and lines of authority are changed frequently, members find it difficult to cope with the resulting stress, and sharp, bitter conflicts can easily erupt over seemingly trivial problems. This type of conflict is generally intense, but it dissipates quickly once a change becomes routinised, and individuals' stress levels are lowered.

3.11.3 Integrative models

The attempt to study the conflict and ways of dealing with the conflicts were attempted using integrative models by many authors. Latham (1996) modelised conflict management by combining the elements of conflict process, underlying environmental structure and behavioural levels of the parties/players. A combination of short term and long term theories of conflict management was also attempted (Thomas, 1992; Latham, 1996). Alternative approaches to conflict management goals based on the beneficiary and time horizon ventures an exceptional model and was protracted by the empirical studies (Thomas, 1992; Lewicki, 1985). *Co-ordination – conflict model* suggests an active intervention when perceptions and the feelings about a situation got distorted and requires stimulation or even resolution approaches to be exercised (Buchanan & Hucynski, 1997). A combination of personality factors (Thomas, 1992; Rahim, 1986), coordination requirements (Kanter, 1997), organisational effectiveness (Victor, 1989) and better human relationship maintenance were all integrated with the dynamics of conflict management.

3.11.4 Process models

The conflict process refers to the sequence of events that occurs during a conflict and the manner in which earlier events cause later events and outcomes and thus necessitating interventions at various levels. Models of the conflict process necessarily incorporate a number of general assumptions about human behaviour, although these assumptions are often implicit. Causal dynamics of sociopathic, normative considerations, morality and ethical issues are some of the major determinants in these models. Fishbein model (1963) which has been extensively tested in a variety of contexts views behaviour as resulting from intentions and sees intentions as shaped by the additive effects of two forms of reasoning-rational/instrumental reasoning and normative reasoning. Fishbein model is basically cognitive and enhanced by Pondy's conflict episode model (1967) inculcating the value of emotions in a conflict phenomenon. Fishbein and Ajzen (1975) have operationalised an individual's overall normative assessment of an act as the product of the perceived endorsement of the act by a given reference group and the individual's motivation to comply or identification with that group's views, summed across reference groups. Other researchers have commented on the need to add the individual's own normative standards to this equation, as in the original Fishbein formulation. This is equivalent to the common practice in role theory of regarding the focal person as receiving a sent role from the self as well as other members of one's role set affecting wider implications on the conflict management mechanism.

3.11.5 Multi dimensional models

Putnam (1988), Pickering (1989) among others critiqued the two dimensional model of conflict handling from the point of view of communication. Three levels of behavioural constructs were dealt in these models, all of which, in retrospect, involved intentions-orientations, strategic objectives, and tactical intentions. The first two of these are collapsed into strategic intentions and tactical intentions were relabeled as tactical intentions (Thomas, 1992). Orientations were in effect a kind of outcome preference, based on one's valence for his own and the other's concerns in the tradition of the dual concerns model.

Strategic objectives were also based on the perceived feasibility of different outcomes, in essence the instrumentality of attempting to achieve those outcomes. Simpler schemes were derived by Greenhalgh (1987), Masterbroek (1980), and Norem-Habeisen and Johnson (1981) implementing cooperative and confrontational behaviour models. In effect, these schemes appear to collapse or omit some of the strategic intentions in the two-dimensional models. In this connection, Rahim and Van de Vliert's (1989) suggestion that the strategic intentions available to a party may in fact simplify to trichotomies and dichotomies as a conflict escalates. Based on conflict perceived and interaction oriented, an individual opts for a strategy believed to be suitable for a particular situation. This may be called strategy attempted.

Based on the presence and absence of these factors, conflict management strategies were constructed in four possible ways (Fogler and Poole, 1984) or six ways (Barclay, 1991).There appear to be anomalies in the placement of two strategic intentions, however. The most consistent anomaly is that compromising is seen by the parties as more cooperative than its placement in these models. That is, even though compromising withholds something as well as offering something to the other, it is rated as cooperative, as is accommodating or collaborating (Kabanoff, 1987; Ruble and Thomas, 1976).

The other anomaly is restricted to the party's perception of the other's intentions. In ratings of the other's intentions, competing is seen as significantly lower on the cooperativeness continuum than these models suggests (Vliert, 1989). In other words, in ratings of the other's intentions, competing appears not to be perceived as merely uncooperative, but as more actively hostile. This is not the case in perceptions of one's own intentions.

3.11.6 Gandhian models

Thomas Weber, a great contemporary Gandhian scholar who specialises conflict resolution along Gandhian lines propagated the Message focus theory (Weber.T, 2001), a technique, appropriate in cases where personal needs rather than values or beliefs are the focus of the conflict, which allows one to express underlying conflicts, is called the "I-Message". In interpersonal conflict the initial response is often destructive, taking the form of blame which generally obscures the real issues underlying the conflict. Reformulating negative statements of blame into "I-Messages" (which explain the feelings of the speaker as the result of unacceptable behaviour by the other and give the speaker's perception of the consequences of the behaviour to themselves, rather than the more usual blaming of the other for unacceptable behaviour and its consequences), can aid the clarification of the issues and steer the conflict onto a constructive and cooperative path. "You-Messages" that are very often sent, unlike "I-Messages", tend to provoke resistance and rebellion.

Gandhi's distinctiveness lies in his "ends and means" concept. The nature of ends and means must mutually correspond. Modern conflict resolution *modus operandi* disappoints in not taking such practical Gandhian initiatives. Gandhi's conflict resolution is holistic in nature while other prevalent methods prefer to resolve a conflict in a piecemeal fashion. Gandhi aims for the highest and the best while he settles for the second best practicable option. Indeed, such a Gandhian approach is clearly missing in the modern conflict management techniques. Self-encapsulation can also occur through both ideological restraints and tactical approach. If at least one of the parties to the conflict develops an ideology that by its very nature limits the weaponry and violence used in the conflict, it is in an important sense self-encapsulating. Mahatma Gandhi's satyagraha (a word taken from Sanskrit, meaning "insistence on truth") movement in the first half of this century used such techniques, and other movements for social justice and self determination have developed variations on this theme of nonviolent direct action.

Perhaps the most obvious self-limiting aspect of Gandhi's confrontation style was its step-wise rather than spiraling escalation. Each satyagraha campaign involved a series of steps, each more challenging to the opponent than the preceding one. It would begin with negotiation and arbitration. This would be an extremely elaborate and lengthy stage including (1) on-site accumulation and analysis of facts, with opponent participation; (2) identification of interests in common with opponents; (3) formulation of a limited action goal acceptable to all parties and mutual discussion of same; and (4) a search for compromise without ceding on

4.1 GANDHIAN APPROACHES

In order to ascertain various mechanisms related with the conflict management approaches, a referential scanning of the same was explored in the focus group and expert panel sessions. Most of the focus group participants and expert panel members were unable to differentiate the pattern of conflict management prescribed and practiced by Mahatma Gandhi. In this regard content analysis of Gandhian literature was attempted along the lines of Gandhian approach to conflict management. It can be observed that the integral approach which revolves around the life principles along with various conflict management techniques leads the Gandhian way. Gandhian experiments of integral approach to conflict management were vividly represented in Ahmedabad textile mill struggle in early 1920s. Mohandas Karamchand Gandhi (2 October 1869 – 30 January 1948) was the pre-eminent political and spiritual leader of India and the Indian independence movement. He was the pioneer of *satyagraha*; resistance to tyranny through mass civil disobedience, firmly founded upon *ahimsa* or total non-violence—which led India to independence and inspired movements for civil rights and freedom across the world. Mahatma Gandhi's thoughts and deeds on human relations and his approach to the conflict handling seem to be one of the guiding lights for modern day managers. Gandhian approach and the practice of managing conflicts are studded with his own personal situations which sometimes can have its linkages through the elements of history, organisational, industrial as well as greater inner conscience. Conflicts, struggles, and fights—all are words used when two or more people have what Gandhi describes as differing "angles of vision" or underlying principles. Gandhi believed that conflict could be resolved by "satyagraha", or "truth force". This concept by operationally stating that in each confrontation lies, "in some measure, truths from each view". "Satyagraha attempts to find a new position, more inclusive than the old ones, to move into it" as was proclaimed by Mahatma through his words and deeds. This type of handling conflicts synthesises positions and is therefore superior to others such as forced victory, accommodation and compromise, and arbitration and law, because ostensibly there are no losers. However Satyagraha does not offer certainty—it only provides a license to visualise, accept and prepare for truth. A larger discussion of what truth is; violence and struggle, coercion, recalcitrant opponents, strength, and the power of non-cooperation are all greatly intertwined with the situational variables. Gandhi said that the root of every Violence and or Conflict is *Untruth* and that the only permanent solution of Conflict is *Truth*.

The prism of Gandhian principles gives much impetus to the interpersonal conflicts and its management in the organisational sphere of life. In this regard the applications of Mahatma's philosophies on the conflict handling are spiraling in nature with its epicenter on the conflicts perceived by individuals. When interpersonal conflicts arise, whether they be between parties having differing degrees of authority (Boss-Subordinate) or between parties having theoretically equal power (Manager-Manager/Directors, Worker-Worker) the general ways of bringing conflicts to an end are for the parties to attempt to impose their will on each other, for authority figures to exercise their authority, or for one party to give in. The first of these "zero-sum" approaches, tilted towards authoritarian options may produce resentment and hostility in the loser, provide them with little motivation to carry out the solution, requires heavy enforcement, inhibits the growth of self-responsibility, self-discipline and creativity, fosters dependence and submission , and may make the winner feel guilty.

Gandhiji does not want to include the permissiveness into his ideas on handling conflicts. This approach (permissiveness) is of the "Okay-you-win, I-give-up" method of dealing with conflict. In the winner this may foster selfishness and reduce their respect for the loser. For the loser it fosters resentment towards the winner, makes them feel guilty about not getting their needs met and may require the loser to be pushed into an authoritarian approach. In these conflict situations those without power or authority learn to cope by rebelling, retaliating, dishonesty (lying, cheating, blaming others, etc.), submitting or even fantasising and regressing. Gandhiji believed that the use of these zero-sum methods will generally lead the manifest conflicts into non compliance situations or sometimes intensive struggle where the parties have unequal power. Where the parties are of relatively equal power, zero-sum methods often result in bitter stalemates making cooperative methods of solving disputes in these circumstances perhaps even more important. Gandhian approaches which are based upon cooperativeness and principled conflict management avoid these negative outcomes.The role-reversal technique of switching viewpoints- where each party honestly tries to argue for the other's viewpoint while the other listens, was also explored by Weber. These techniques are also applicable for organisational/industrial situations where there is a sufficient degree of rapport. Further the techniques of 'active-listening' and 'mirroring' could be used until hearing what the opponent in a conflict is saying becomes second nature. The essence of active listening is mirroring back what has been said. This assures the accuracy of listening and also assures the sender that he has been understood when he hears his own message fed back to him accurately.

Active listening can help to solve immediate interpersonal conflicts or it can be used by a third party to help one of the antagonists in a conflict situation clarify their own feelings and think creatively about possible solutions.

The visualisations of the management of conflicts were attempted by many practitioners all over the globe. The influence of Gandhian philosophy of Satyagraha, Win-Win and non-zero sum game as well as the proactive conflict dynamics are all fine-tuned for organisational adaptations by Mark Juergensmeyer who had postulated the under mentioned ten basic rules along the Gandhian lines for handling conflicts (Mark Juergensmeyer,2004).

1) Do not avoid confrontation. Avoidance simply prolongs underlying conflicts. Encounters between positions bring clarity.

2) Stay open to communication and self-criticism. Critical perspective is needed to sort out truth from untruth.

3) Find a resolution and hold fast to it. Seize onto harmonious alternatives, but be willing to challenge and change them.

4) Regard your opponent as a potential ally. Do nothing to harm or alienate your opponent. Your goal is to join forces to struggle against untruth.

5) Make your tactics consistent with your goal.

6) Be flexible. Be willing to change tactics, alter goals, and revise notions, including those of your opponent and your conception of truth.

7) Be temperate. Escalate your actions by degrees. Opponents should not feel intimidated, thereby fostering communication rather than defensiveness.

8) Be proportionate. Determine trivial vs. important issues. The basis for judgment is the degree to which life and the quality of life are abused. Mount a campaign of strength equal to that of the opponent.

9) Be disciplined. Especially when involving large numbers for collective action. Make certain your position is coherent, consistent, and committed to nonviolence.

10) Know when to quit. Deadlocked campaigns or ones with negative results may require revision in tactics or a change of goals. Concession, without agreement on principle is not victory. Victory can only be claimed with both sides can say the same.

Conflicts, according to Gandhiji are only a clash of interest and opinions, and are not the real problem. There will always be different thoughts and ideas among organisational citizens. According to him, there is surely a beauty in this. Further he agrees that the question is not conflict itself; it is how individuals handle conflict.

There are only two ways – through violence or through nonviolence. If conflict is handled properly they can lead to growth in institutions, they can lead to growth in personal relationships. Of course Gandhi did not know of these techniques by these names; however, he was fond of emphasising the need for caring and cooperative interpersonal relations that these techniques may aid to achieve. He firmly believed that the home was the training ground of Satyagraha--that it was the world in microcosm and how we reacted to aggression from strangers or handled our disagreement with them depended upon that training. The care and attention paid to small seemingly unimportant conflicts is as important as that given larger disputes, for it will be by those small things that the organisations shall be judged. These techniques can be applied in the modern day business units and its dynamic individuals.

Gandhiji pioneered what is now called as the win-win approach to conflict management and shed some light to evaluate conflict from a win-win perspective. The techniques that he incorporated in his life can then be applied to the goal of demonstrating pitfalls and potential positive outcomes. Winning in the Gandhian sense, requires a transformation of relationships. Win-Win sees life as a cooperative, not a competitive arena. Most people tend to think in terms of dichotomies- strong or weak, win or lose. But that kind of thinking is fundamentally flawed, because it is based on power and position rather than principle. Win-Win means that agreements or solutions are mutually beneficial and mutually satisfying. With a Win-Win solution, all parties feel good about the decision and feel committed to the action plan. In one of his manifold dialogues, Gandhiji equates the winning approaches to the chariot of Rama in Ramayana. The armed chariot that wins the victory of Rama in Ramayana is not of the ordinary kind- "Courage is its wheels; character its banner; self discipline and good will its horses, with mercy and spiritual balance as its reins."

4.2 MARY PARKER FOLLETT AND INTEGRATIVE PATHS OF CONFLICT MANAGEMENT

Managerial in-depth interviews had revealed that conflict management techniques can and should be applied to any one or more of the combination of conflict management approaches in a holistic way. Content analysis was explored regarding the combined conflict management approaches and in this regard integrative conflict management approach prescribed by Mary Parker Follett (1868-1933) was put into analysis. This was supplemented by the inputs from in-depth interview sessions and focus group interviews. It was observed that the multi-track approach, working at different levels has for sometime already been practiced in both micro and meso levels in the organisational sector. Unraveling false perceptions, allowing distorted perception mechanisms to be cleared and hardened concepts to be dissolved is an option to worth considering. By examining alternative modes of action as well as by reviewing one's own patterns of behaviour can also be a positive step towards this direction for the individual concerns. It was observed from various sessions of in-depth interviews that for better managing the content-level conflicts; managers must take step necessary to collect and straightening out the various themes in a conflict and look at them more precisely. Managers must learn rather trained to recognise their own distinct behaviour patterns and role expectations, to review these and to adapt them to the given situation. Good and active cooperation, prescriptive principles and stringent rules should be formulated to avoid any anomalies concerning procedural level conflicts.

Managers indicated that managerial degree of uncertainty should be minimal to the extent. Co-knowledge or co-decisions in co-determination policy issues lessens the conflict that caused by external relations as well as aroused by procedural dynamics of the team concerned. Work in the group environment can be enhanced if the teams and their leaders will participate actively in the process of recognising and identify the higher team dynamics. Managers and team leaders have put forward a number of basic tools in focus group sessions that allow for rapid diagnosis of the strengths and weaknesses of each of the five key levels of team functioning as well as their influence on each other. This work to be done is by its nature interdisciplinary and touches the concepts of major behavioural sciences. The maintenance of the appropriate conflict level in the organisational scenario is carried out by various interventions. One of the major conscious interventions to stimulate conflict level is dialectic method followed in executive and general body meetings. Fostering a debate of opposing viewpoints to better understand an issue is dealt with in this method. Thoughts are taken as thoughts rather than giving undue importance to it as his/their thoughts or my thoughts in its minimal sphere.

Mary Parker Follett expressed that *"the very act of solving a conflict was not static, but part of the dynamic and continuous pattern of circular response which characterises all human activities."* Through her books titled *Creative experience* and *Dynamic administration*, she had advocated that in an encounter between A and B, B does not merely react to what A does. He also reacts to his own anticipation of what A may do on his own and of how A may react to what B does. Mary Parker Follett's memorable lines could as well be repeated, *"The conception of circular behaviour throws much light on conflicts for now I realise that I can never fight you. I am always fighting you plus me. I have put it this way—that response is always to a relation. I respond not only to you but to the relation between you and me."* In the conflict management process, there is always a scope for a revaluation of interests and a revaluation of desires leading to a realignment of groups thereby retransformation of conflict potentialities.

Managers agreed that conflict management at its core enshrines functional cooperation by and through the pooling of organisational talents. May be conflict management refers to all conscious dynamic interventions that enables to promote a sustainable conflict intensity level which stems out of transitional or transformational process at the given settings. Focus group sessions had indicated that this organisational adventure must actively envision, include, respect and promote the human and cultural resources of the organisation. Managers and few executives are also of the opinion that this involves a new set of the understanding through which they do not often see the setting and the people in it as the *problem* and *the solution* as the sole answer. Rather they understand the long-term goal of transformatary values as validating and building on people and resources of business organisations.

Most of the sessions indicated that conflict is part of every organisation and the managers do recognise it. A conflict manager being a transformational leader has a high level of comfort with managing dissent and conflict in their organisations. These leaders nurture conflict within their organisations believing that out of conflict, innovation occurs. May be a lesson or two from the Gandhian approach of dealing conflicts can serve its purpose for the future managerial interventions. The basis for dealing with conflict and disagreement originate out of a genuine appreciation of the differences between people that our Indian culture is very often sighted for. To become genuine conflict (transformational) leaders, the managers have to undergone self-transformation; rather they are transforming themselves to greater heights and influencing / facilitating transformational values on their followers. In short, conflict managers transformed as value-based leaders creates an atmosphere of trust and openness with his willingness to tell it *like it is* and thereby transforming the conflicts to its rightful managerial heights. Probably self-transformations, value based principles, organisational openness, and consciousness of functional cooperation fits the initial ingredients for the adorable list of conflict management.

The organisational efforts and initiatives should make an employee feel that the company values his past contributions, and wants him to have a fulfilling and positive attitude towards work. To prevent boredom, monotony at work, and burnt out employees are eager to pursue hobbies and interests. At times, this can be given more priority and thus effect an individual's concentration at work as practiced by the HRM for dealing with Raman's problems. The capability to identify the various skills in an organisation rests with the managers. Therefore, they have to demonstrate behaviours that help nurture employees' skills. Personal aspirations play significantly influences an individual's performance at work. People tend to work better to fulfill personal aspirations rather than duty or obligation. However, obstacles like ill health or circumstances often prevent the realisation of a dream. People who were successful and were excellent performers may never have had a dream to work towards. Despite success and fame, such employees never have anything more to look forward to. They do not put in the time, energy and talent that they once used to. Resonance makes them reflect on work and how they can make it more meaningful.

Low-conflict organisations and Conflict Management

Low-conflict organisations are not simply characterised by the absence of features possessed by high-conflict organisations. Three companies in the sampled structure are apparently identified intuitively aided with the perceptive assimilation as low-conflict organisations and an attempt was made to pattern the elements that are unique and differentiative with the rest of the group as per the guided revealing from the middle managers in those organisations. The low conflict organisation and its patterns of cooperation can and should be described and discussed in terms of its own practices and internal dynamics. It is also important to note that the low-conflict organisations are not without disputes and differences; rather, the differences, which arise, are managed in a way that avoids extreme rancour, polarisation, and outright violent expressions. Low -conflict organisations have a psycho-cultural environment that is affectionate, warm, low in overt aggression, and relatively untroubled by aggressive and zero sum conflicts. Dispositions established in the earlier phases of organisational life through conscious training and open communication channels build organisational ontology that foster the peaceful management of differences. These dispositions engender a low level of overt conflict, so that there are few models of violent action and reinforcing the idea that nonviolent action can be efficacious. Disputes in low-conflict organisations can be intense and bitter, but they are less likely to escalate into violence and destruction, which make constructive solutions harder to achieve.

Certainly anger and frustration may be accompanied by displacement, projection, and externalisation. But in the end these emotions are less intense because conflicts are not felt as threats to the fundamental existence of oneself or the group. Low-conflict organisations are the most likely places to find constructive conflict management because the psycho cultural dispositions are most conducive to creative joint problem solving and open communication. The chances to find a few low-conflict settings where conflict management is not constructive in these organisations are unavoidable, partially because low levels of conflict can occur when one party is more powerful than the other and the weaker party is unable to press its case effectively. Examination of particular cases reveals important stylistic differences among constructive conflicts in these organisations as well as shared characteristics. A common pattern seems to be that the goals of conflict management are often quite diffuse and subjective. Even while disputants are in conflict, they seem to have a strong sense of linked fate. As a result, conflict management often develops a strong orientation towards the future in which parties do not emphasise short-term concerns as much as long-term relationships. In fact, these organisations seem to resist focusing exclusively on the narrow substance of a dispute and instead pay attention to the larger organisational context in which it is embedded. This provides a way to avoid responding to hostile actions of others with reciprocal, mutually hostile acts that set off escalatory spirals throughout the organisational understanding. Training and developmental module in these organisations are ever dynamic and it seems that they had an immense effect on the conflict level felt among the organisational elements. This not only shows the training and developmental module acting as per the bookish measures; rather addressing or elevating the issues concerned to the levels of personalised mentoring with its manifold influential spheres.

Low level of aggression is promoted by both low permissiveness and strict self-control among the managerial workforce in these organisations. Organisational conformity apparently makes punishment unnecessary, for individuals and groups often monitor themselves in a manner that collectively suits best for the organisation. Most of the middle level managers connect the low levels of conflict in these organisations to a deep collective sense of responsibility and emphasised the noneconomic aspects of relationships as part of the strong sense of group/ related groups. The sense of psycho-social responsibility is expressed in a variety of ways – a strong emphasis on equality and leveling, attentiveness to group/organisational norms, a great degree of conformity, and a high level of participation even without necessarily high personal commitment. There is, simultaneously, a profound concern for the welfare of others and a certain emotional reserve in personal relations.

Tremendous care is taken not to hurt the feelings of others. Despite their interpersonal sensitivity and reserve, however, the managers in these organisations have little suspicion of top level executives or their fellow subordinates and they do not believe that others will take advantage of them. They perceived that the organisation is there for all, if and when it is needed. Decision-making and the exercise of authority in these organisations are intended to keep overt conflict low and discuss the expressed conflicts in non-confrontative and positive ways. Local/departmental decision-making often involves extensive private/in-group discussion to reach consensus prior to organisational/broader consideration. Broad-based coalitions are valued and regularly sought, and when consensus cannot be reached, matters are often dropped. Finally, managerial advises /interventions make much of legalism and formalism as a way of removing an issue from controversy by standardising the ways in which tasks are performed. What is more, these organisations have not known any upheaval or violent changes in its institutional makeup (they welcomed and rapidly embraced the technical requisites) since the advent of liberalised and globalised scenario from 1991, changes that might otherwise have caused a shift in core values. On the contrary, continuation and tradition plays an important role to promote conscious / quasi-intended conflict managerial momentum.

Core values and behavioural norms

Individual companies are part of wider business sphere of activities among conglomerates in many cases. The centralised managerial culture and the corporate commanding by the parent company or the influential persons of the parent company may cast a deeper impact in the managerial activities of the managers concerned. Middle level managers of KM Ltd, being part of the wider conglomerate KMR group, faced an academically pertinent conflict situation in recent time. The core values concerning *integrity*, triggered substantial conflict during its transmission from the parent group to the concerned organisation, especially among the managerial workforce. The normative component of this organisational practice demands the abstinence of all employees group wide from any activity that is illegal or violates fair trade. It specifies concrete behavioural rules concerning price fixing, collusive tendering and corruption, and includes, among others, an unwritten but substantially stressed point against the reception or granting of personal gifts to and from customers, suppliers or state/other organisations. Regarding the latter issue, the interviewees (managers) described the value of integrity as clashing with their own local business traditions which are firmly rooted in societal normative institutions.

A long history of the concerned organisation's tradition demands and allows the regular exchange of gifts, sometimes rather valuable items, between partners of a relationship, in this case between the company's sales personnel and local customers and suppliers. The ritual has a high symbolic value for business people/clients. And, in the cultural context of the particular organisation, it is explicitly *not* perceived as being associated with illegal practices or corruption but as an indispensable and socially highly acceptable gesture of politeness that strengthens the bonds between business partners. As such, the practice is interpreted by the managers as being an important basis of good business relationships and as contributing to local business success. Consequently, two highly diverse patterns of meaning and interpretation collide in this practice. As reported by managers, this situation leads to a dilemma for the local sales staff and opens up a double field of conflict. If the sales personnel adhere to the norms set by the parent company, they risk a conflict with their current /potential business partners. In fact, person from the sales team recalls an instance where the prescribed regulation has led to unpleasant debates and embarrassing situation with a particular client who perceived the rejection of gifts offered as being rude and as harming the mutual relationship. If managers in turn sticks with the past tradition and his/her own internalised norms, conflict potential is generated between him and a local/parent upper management which is responsible for implementation of the practice and needs to legitimise its own doings vis-à-vis the corporate headquarter. Even though the threat is perceived as being rather diffuse, noncompliance can, according to the interviewed managers, potentially lead to poor evaluations in management appraisal procedures and thus damage the personal career outlook. The managers perceived the conflict potential generated at the subsidiary to be substantial. It took them more than one year to handle the conflict in a way satisfactory to both parties; the managers, especially from sales team and the corporate headquarters. During this process the original practice associated with the integrity-value has been altered considerably.

Human resource manager with the help of Vice President initiated a series of talks and workshops to identify the exact causes of conflict and to understand the employees' ideas, attitudes and individual interests regarding the core value transferred to the organisation concerned. As a result, the behavioural standards as determined by the parent company have been readjusted through the formulation of a joint interpretation of the value guidelines and compromised amendments regarding acceptability and legitimacy of single, precisely defined activities in local operations.

It was approved in principle that gifts offered to customers or suppliers are acceptable if they are taken from a predefined pool of corporate presents in order to allow for continuation of traditional local rituals. Gifts can be received when they are below a certain value and when they are not brought to personal use of the respective person. Instead, the company had established an annual procedure where through lottery or auction the presents collected over the year are redistributed among all employees. The issue caused some interim damage to the relationship between the company and its local environment (customers, suppliers) but, according to managers, the compromise implemented is acceptable to all involved. Intra-personal effects include feelings of insecurity and dissonance between internalised norms and behavioural patterns and those imposed by the parent company during the conflictual period but the structural process effectively helps to reduce these individual uncertainties. The frequency of use and the reporting received by the human resource director indicate a positive reception of the structure by employees. Although the issue was amicably solved, it bears an appropriate application of the unwritten procedure-a loophole that can distort compared to a well written rule or the standard. Further workforce favours guided procedure in this particular case, rather than a well written rule, which always brings elements of vagueness with it because of the uncertainty it got attached.

Quality standards and Active avoidance tactics

In the production department of PFL Ltd, an interesting conflict occurs when the top level management initiated to impose a quality plan. In this production department, quality is a highly value-infused issue going far beyond mere product specifications. A supreme quality as such is heavily loaded with symbolic meaning, generating pride and identification of the workers involved in its production process. In this unit, this quality orientation has led to an ever improved refinement of product features and the development of specific production technology over time. The recent restructuration into global business units, however, is accompanied by top managerial efforts to globally re-align product specifications and production technologies in order to provide its global customers with exactly the same quality wherever they demand the product and, even more importantly, to reduce costs of technology adaptation and to strengthen the global joint production and delivery system in the long run. For this unit, the introduction of these global quality standards would entail the actual reduction of local product quality in the long run, where the local interests in continuous improvement of quality and its high inherent symbolic value clash with the parent company's interests of global standardisation, conflict is generated.

To handle this conflict the production department, especially production manager and quality control staffs pursued a tactic of deceleration. The issue was infrequently discussed by the company meetings and managers have successfully avoided the implementation of the restructured quality standards. Managers discussed different reasons for this course of events-First, the stable performance of the concerned department as perceived to be a key argument against any enforced changes of local processes. In addition, the geographical distance and peripheral position of the potential buyer and communication system prevents or at least delays direct interference of the official dealings regarding yarn specifications. So far, headquarters have not established any formal platforms for discussion and enforcement of the practice transfer like a task force or special appointee. The departmental staff proved to be right in choosing to adhere to *their* policies which were instrumental to obtain a highly profitable order from a much bigger and long term serving global client who had backed the quality standards solely because of the track record of continuous improvement in production quality and standards of the concerned organisation.

Myth of 360 degree solutions to conflicts

The case of Mr. Ramamurthy, SMP Ltd provides an opportunity to understand causes of conflict situations in business organisations, and ways and means of managing such situations. The conflict discussed in the case is not uncommon in a business unit. Often such conflicts remain unresolved, creating adverse organisational effects. They influence team-work and affect desired outputs. While managerial team would like to find a congenial solution to such conflicts, they are often difficult to handle.

The letter from the production department was very strong. It concluded by observing; *"If this is the attitude of the sales department, we shall have no collaboration with them as of now. Not only do they lack a healthy attitude towards collaborative work, they have often refused to share achievements. Now they want to stifle our work on product specifications, notwithstanding the fact that we have been working on its continuous improvement for over a decade. We would of course continue our work in this area, but without the undue interference of sales department."* Mr. Ramamurthy, Human resource manager, put down the letter and was quite annoyed. He had known that there was trouble between the sales and production departments, or rather between two senior managers of these departments. He had not expected it to reach this level. There had been several instances of conflicts between the managers and their divisions, but the conflicts had never reached boiling point.

They were usually resolved amicably, even before the higher authorities took note of them. Mostly the conflicts arose over allocation of funds for product packaging, budgetary allocations and participation in company representations in external meetings/conferences. However the present conflict is at its face value, without a series motive except the individuals/personal conflict between the two senior managers in the sales and production departments. Further, the conflict between the production and sales departments was different. It was a conflict between two departments which had always collaborated in the past. It was a conflict between two senior managers who had worked together on the same problem over a decade, and had jointly arrived at a solution to improve the products' quality and acceptability. For some strange reason, friends had become foes. In the process, they had vitiated to some extent the environment of the organisation.

Ramamurthy hardly discussed these issues consciously and he perceived that the friendly relations between him and sales manager would become abstemious if he does so. In the mean time, the conflict spreads to greater heights and the two departmental staffs *provoked* by their respective heads, made serious complaints blaming other department to the Managing Director in lieu the rejection of the export order causing time delay. Ramamurthy was at cross roads when the Managing Director put the blame of avoiding the known sparkles of conflict in the past at him and made confrontational meetings with all departmental managers including sales, production. Majority of the managers were seriously disturbed by this confrontational attitude of the authority and blamed in more civilised terms about the aversive/indifferent attitude of human resource department to solve issues like that between *certain individuals*.

Ramamurthy held a series of meetings with sales and production managers individually as well as collectively and put in strong words that the situation was becoming serious and counseled them invoking how they benefitted by their friendly relationship in the past and how they are viewed by their departmental staff as of now. Further he presented the loss suffered by the company because of their strained relationship. A combination of perceived threat with the other, disparities in case of monetary benefit accruals, familial problems related to each other(they being relatives) and a differentiative treatment they are offered by top officials were unfolded among others that points the hidden motives behind the strained relationship. A pragmatic and a touching counsel from Ramamurthy enabled the two managers to put aside the differences and to be their productive heights.

Ramamurthy was satisfied with the results he achieved but asserts that he should have avoided the ugly outburst by staffs and related things that followed by initiating to find a solution in the earlier periods of the interpersonal conflict among the two departmental managers. *"Every conflict cannot be solved. The seeds of potential conflicts are embedded sometimes in the organisational system itself and perpetuated by not only by top officials but also by other employees of the organisation"*, he asserted.

The individual personalities as well as their perceptions, concepts and ideas, emotions, intentions and behaviours are major sources of conflict in this case and Human resource manager's focus here was on the topic and on the task to be performed to amicably settle the issue that he fails to respond in the initial days. For a better handling of the issue, the mutual attitudes of the group members are important, as well as the state of relations between them and the interaction climate, roles and behavioural patterns. Here, techniques of problem solving in a team-such as analytic methods, decision making methods, creativity techniques, formal internal rules for the team and the use of auxiliary means are partially beyond the control of the human resource manager. Further, the way in which information and contacts are cultivated with the rest of the organisation including the rules regarding delegation of work, monetary benefits, if attempted to alter strategically may invite serious issues with various quarters. The best that can be arrived is to provide a decent hearing and active listening by which situation becomes atleast normal if not highly positive. The admixture of conflict management approaches in a theoretical framework starting from controlling the conflict up to reasonably transform or atleast to try to transform the issue got experienced by Ramamurthy and it exposes the most relevant fact that a conflict cannot be completely solved with a 360 degree satisfaction of all the parties as the path of moving from one level of conflict to another/others was experienced by the parties of conflict.

Managing Reactionary impulses

Kumar seems to be learnt a lesson or two from his recent experience which resulted in the reactionary impulses between two conflicting parties and the collateral effects that followed. *"Don't come and try to tell me often what to do!"*– Mani, one of the supervisor bristled when Kumar, production in charge of SRMP Ltd tried to initiate an open dialogue to find a reasonable solution to a conflict existing between Mani, supervisor who has a conflict prone history and a group of workmen including Hari, a sincere and long serving employee. The reason behind the outburst of Mani was well known as he wants to be shifted to another department (quality control/headquarters-testing) and was immensely dissatisfied with his present position. Kumar agreed that Mani had the required exposure and qualification to get a post in his mind but an array of problems persist which can be attributed to vested interests of some higher officials to install another candidate from outside to the same position. In this time, Kumar feels that Mani was not to be blamed and the situation reasonably points fault with Hari among others, he got irritated by a provocative attitude of Mani. In the mean time, Hari and others complained about their supervisor's attitude and dealings with the higher authorities without consulting Kumar. The matter had become serious and exaggerated out of proportion as described by the respondents and Mani was served with a memo by Factory manager, the date when Kumar was on leave.

Kumar was at crossroads and extremely unhappy the way situation was handled by authorities and the parties. He convincingly and assertively reasoned out his displeasure directly to the factory manager and told the dynamics of the conflict in greater detail between the parties. A meeting was convened with necessary departmental staff and the conflicting parties –Hari and Mani. The meeting ended with a stern oral warning to Hari and a well balanced approach that they had taken the concerns expressed by him. Mani had reacted very negatively and indifferent in the meeting, although he expressed his desire to get a transfer that he is qualified and eagerly waits. Further, he apologised for the remarks that he made during his conversations with Kumar. The proceedings called off by the factory manager with a settlement reached. Meanwhile, Kumar insisted that there should be a representation addressing Mani's genuine concerns and all the members agreed the same. Two weeks passed out and on a sudden day Mani came to Kumar's chamber and handed over his resignation letter. Kumar got shocked and enquired about his reason for leaving and Mani explained about non committal attitude of his genuine aspirations and a harsh response he received from the authorities. Kumar took this matter and collateral happenings to the Managing Director along with Human resource manager and find an embarrassing response from him. Managing Director revealed that the company was interested to recruit persons from a particular competitive company for their quality control department, the reasons beyond explanation and cannot accommodate Mani there and factory manager was directed to accept Mani's resignation. Interestingly, after a few days Kumar got an opportunity to meet Mani in a public place and had a brief conversation while Mani told about his recent job as a quality control specialist in a competitive unit of Kumar's and their organisation is in search for a factory manager with a production background . Kumar in his private conversation told he is still not averse to Mani's information.

Conflict management in these days is shifting from its traditional spheres and middle level managers are at the cross roads. A reasonable facilitative platform to strengthen employees sense of self, to increase their confidence that they are taken seriously by others as beings with a history, an identity worthy of respect and needs that must be addressed and to treat them in ways that honor and support their own resources for making decisions and pursuing solutions to their problems and need-satisfaction is the need of hour in many cases. In this case an ever damaging operational mechanism revolving around the unavailable measures in a satisfactory way can be a serious cause of the attrition. Further, the pattern shows that if it got unaddressed may cause serious damage to the organisational activities. Middle level managers are expected to bridge the conflict managerial measures. The spiraling and multiplex nature of conflicts explained in this case shows that even managers are in great need to address several conflicts effectively and it got vitiated by the unavailability of the organisational procedures and related mechanisms.

Workplace cold wars and hot options

Mahesh took charge as factory manager of GDK (P) Ltd, a job he deserved in his previous unit but was constantly rejected. Being a man from Human resource stream, naturally he started his new operations with the human resource department and arranged a staff meeting with all important staffs from all departments. To his surprise, the meeting was unusually cold and no serious discussions were held between the participants except occasional exchanges of premeditated/crafted words. In later days, Mahesh realised that senior managers in almost all departments are indifferent with each other's affairs and they had only occasional task related interactions. The deeper query points out that relative isolation and an over dose of distorted information of departments were promoted by previous board and Directors. Mahesh discussed the matter in a friendly way with the current Managerial authorities and got a positive feedback from them to enable a wider human participation.

Mahesh convened a meeting with all the important staffs and stressed the need to have a deeper relationship among the departments, besides the task related cooperation that is to be put to new heights. To his utter surprise, human resource manager treated the message as provocative and directly put against him/his inability. It was shot back by the short tempered response from the sales personnel. The situation was controlled by the right intervention from other managers. Mahesh realised that volcano which was silent got erupted and thought about the right steps to put the situation under control.

Mahesh personally met the two problematic managers in their respective chambers and disclosed his real intentions and sternly warns about their misbehaviours. Later, those particular sales personnel along with human resource manager and production manager were put to charge as members of task force to implement quality improvement groups in the unit by Mahesh. Mahesh was particularly tough in the timely introduction of quality groups and extracted good work from all spheres. Factory Manager was perceived as strict and tough to beat by many managers through this process. In his address in one of the review meeting, he showered praises to the task force members and won great acclaim while announcing a token reward to the taskforce. The entire workforce was thrilled as they were unheard of these kinds of gestures in the past and made every effort to enable quality groups a real success.

Although, the company got mixed benefits by the introduction of quality groups, the interaction among the workforce were put into new heights. Mahesh describe that team building is creating a work culture that values collaboration. In a teamwork environment, people understand and believe that thinking, planning, decisions and actions are better when done cooperatively. People recognise, and even assimilate, the belief that *"none of us is as good as all of us. You can, however, create a teamwork culture by doing just a few things right. Admittedly, they're the hard things, but with commitment and appreciation for the value, you can create an overall sense of teamwork in your organisation"*, he added reflecting an aura of transformational leadership in managing conflicts.

Managing conflicts through consensus building

Groups often collaborate closely in order to reach consensus or agreement. The ability to use collaboration requires the recognition of and respect for everyone's ideas, opinions, and suggestions. Consensus requires that each participant must agree on the point being discussed before it becomes a part of the decision. *"Not every point will meet with everyone's complete approval. Unanimity is not the goal. The goal is to have individuals accept a point of view based on logic. When individuals can understand and accept the logic of a differing point of view, you must assume you have reached consensus"*, remarked Mr.Pramod of SKT Ltd., production in charge an effective team manager. He along with his team members had a tactical guideline to manage conflicts and to build consensus. He usually follows and prescribes these guidelines for reaching consensus -

- Avoid arguing over individual ranking or position. Present a position as logically as possible.
- Avoid "win-lose" statements. Discard the notion that someone must win.

- Avoid changing of minds only in order to avoid conflict and to achieve harmony.

- Avoid majority voting, averaging, bargaining, or coin flipping. These do not lead to consensus. Treat differences of opinion as indicative of incomplete sharing of relevant information, keep asking questions.

- Keep the attitude that holding different views is both natural and healthy to a group.

The most important element is to view initial agreement as suspect and exploring the reasons underlying apparent agreement and make sure that members have really/willingly agreed. There are a few key variables that define conflict management situations and determine which conflict management strategies are likely to be effective. Pramod is of the opinion that time pressure is an important variable–if there were never any time pressures, collaboration might always be the best approach to use. In addition to time pressures, some of the most important factors to consider are issue importance, relationship importance, and relative power-

- The extent to which important priorities, principles or values are involved in the conflict.

- How important it is that you maintain a close, mutually supportive relationship with the other party.

- How much power you have compared to how much power other party has.

In search of creative conflict management mode

The choice of conflict management mode is associated with managerial effectiveness. The ability to creatively manage conflict situations, towards constructive outcomes is becoming a standard requirement. Mr. Rajesh, Human resource manager in NM Ltd agrees that, *"While tensions and misunderstandings are normal and inevitable, if left unresolved they result in hostility, stress and wasted resources in the organisations."* He usually follows a broader approach and mange the conflict situation with pre-meditated phases. Once he had been made aware of a relationship problem, he calls a meeting with the people concerned, and defines the situation as factually as possible. At this initial stage, he agrees that it is usually difficult to define facts, so he keeps things as simple as possible and address the issue but not as a problem. He further stresses to confront the possible negative issues in the relationship. He finds out the problems and constraints the two people/parties involved are dealing with and prepares a ground to share their respective views.

He further encourages parties to look at the possible positive sides to their relationship. People have a tendency to treat perceptions as reality thereby moving a few steps closer to finding out what they are looking for from the relationship. At this stage Rajesh begin to visualise to look for possible solutions to their problems, but without asking for any form of commitment yet. Brainstorm the possibilities. Once he had looked at various options, he starts gaining greater commitment from them and generates to integrate the positive concerns and subsequently minimising the negative ones. Then comes the right time to generate directions (strategies) in order to achieve the listed aspirations and a list of combined plans, actions, objectives and supporting goals were prepared collaboratively.

At this juncture, the unsettled negative factors are dealt and the ground becomes green enough to arrive at amicable settlements and emphasising the parties of conflict to greater care and concentration on positive aspects of their relationships. Rajesh further emphasises on the supporting structure (resources, system) to accomplish the aspirations and selected directions. He emphasises that without this structure no idea can move forward. This may simply be a regular scheduled meeting to follow up on actions. Ultimately, he make a decent estimate/Measure the cost of non-compliance (non-adherence). This means ensuring that they are aware of the cost of not following the solution/s (direction and structure) to the problem, and consequently doing whatever is necessary to get the process back on course.

In the next phase, decisions concerning when and how the parties and others are going to evaluate and re-evaluate the decisions taken and the progress that may or may not have been made that creates accountability. In the final phase, summary of the discussions are prepared with an active promotion of positive aspects. He asserts that the whole process can be a well built one if there is a relatively loosened time pressure.

The above case prescribes that a unique and procedural conflict management scenario brings a framework for an efficient conflict management. Further, the ability to manage conflict is a critical skill in the workplace, and has been identified as a core competency for managers and leaders at all levels. It is ironic, therefore, that companies hesitate to invest time and money in improving employees' conflict management abilities when the cost of conflict in financial and other terms can be enormous.

Conscious activation and execution of the research mechanism in terms of data acquisition strategies expressed through the overlapping modules in this study paves way for an exploratory analysis of the data collected in tandem to have a modulating and pragmatic appraisal. Predominantly inclusive analysis inculcating a qualitative exploration stimulated with the error minimisation can be a logical attempt that shall promote an expanded understanding regarding the state of affairs experienced by the study group in organisational settings. Highly interrelated and correlated constituents point to enable summation of a cross-segmental analysis of data acquired through In-depth interviews, Focus Groups, Semi-structured Observations, Content Analysis and Expert/managerial opinions/brainstorming. An appraisal of the *ground reality* through a quasi attempt of scientific triangulations along these lines can be expressed by the term *heuristic appraisal of the conflict management climate.*

In-depth interview sessions with a judgemental sample of human resource clusters from middle-level managers (study group); supervisors and general workers (subordinates of the study group/assistive workforce); corporate executives (superiors/the reporting authority) are sought out in a guided fashion totaling atleast *thirty sessions* representing each clusters. focus group sessions were delineated to the maximum of ten (10) comprising such collections of people as participants from the study group and their organisational co-occupants– top level executives, supervisors, factory workers and others. Prospective participants are approached and those who volunteered for the same were included with a judgemental consideration. Each session got activated for about ninety (90) minutes to the participants ranging between five (5) and nine (9). Every session proceeded adhering to the themes of the research questions with a guided intervention from the part of the facilitator. An active attempt to bridge the gap between the theoretical understanding and the real practices were followed by semi structured observations consciously farmed through out the modules of study. Further content analysis was carried out through permitted organisational documents including reports, diaries /other documentation from the study group and other officials belong to the adorable list of data along the lines of research questions. The predominantly qualitative and explorative data acquired through these modes of operations requires methodological challenge and thus rightly termed as heuristic appraisal of conflict managerial climate, essentially a cautiously optimistic appraisal that helps and attempts to triangulate the resultants asserted through other modes of inquest.

The role of culturally shared, profound *we-they* stand, oppositions, the conceptualisation of enemies and allies, and deep-seated dispositions about human action stemming from earliest development is extremely beyond the scope of the present study, whereas the organisational sparkles bears the potential resultants of them in a variety of ways. Revelations from the managerial population indicates that the conflicts are sometimes just left unsolved, because nothing / nobody can conciliate the two parties, and cases were mentioned where such a situation lasted for years. In one case those involved would go on bickering year in and year out, and in another they chose not to communicate at all. *"...company, at least to my experience, has a fairly soft culture, they care for people, they don't confront people, and that has the consequence that conflicts may live for a very long time"* (Production Manager).Another manager thus hinted, *"There are two other persons here; there is a constant conflict between him/his department and the production department. That has been lasting for about fifteen years or so, and now we are trying to solve it, but it is not that easy. It is much harder now than it was fifteen years ago. Only in the past few years have we realised how deep the conflict really is"* (Operations manager).

6.2 Perceptual conflict asymmetry and its Management

Managers are of the opinion that rarely do two people simultaneously recognise a difference in positions or interests in same degree.   According to them, perceptual conflict composition is the degree to which one person perceives that a conflict is present compared to the other person involved in the conflict. This concept of asymmetry thus examines the differences in perceptions of conflict among the parties involved in the conflict where one person may perceive that a serious conflict exists while the other party believes there is no or a very low level of conflict present. Perceptual asymmetry of conflict is that in an asymmetrical conflict, party A perceives more conflict than party B. Further managers pointed out that when one party believes there is conflict and the other does not, discomfort and inequity will exist between the parties. If put into the logic, this will cause the parties involved in the conflict to be less satisfied than when symmetrical views of the conflict experience exists. In addition to this managers as well as supervisory cadre employees are of the opinion that if party A believes that his view of the situation is not validated by the other party, or party B, he may question her /his own view of the situation. According to self-verification theory, this may decrease motivation, effort, satisfaction, and performance. Individuals search for coherence in their interactions and organisational environment, and inconsistencies can negatively affect the processes and outcomes of the parties involved. This is considered a meta-conflict construct (conflict about conflict), which can influence outcomes such as commitment, cohesiveness, satisfaction, and individual and group performance.

Mary parker Follett expressed that *"the very act of solving a conflict was not static, but part of the dynamic and continuous pattern of circular response which characterises all human activities"*. In an encounter between A and B, B does not merely react to what A does. He also reacts to his own anticipation of what A may do on his own and of how A may react to what B does. Mary parker Follett's memorable lines could as well be repeated, *"The conception of circular behaviour throws much light on conflicts for now I realise that I can never fight you. I am always fighting you plus me. I have put it this way- that response is always to a relation. I respond not only to you but to the relation between you and me"*. An asymmetrical conflict structure exists when one party wants to change the status quo, and the other party wants to keep the status quo as it is. The unfairness that individuals feel can cause decreased motivation, depression, and dissatisfaction with the relationship fuelling spiraling conflicts that are often handled with the obsolete human minds. Interestingly, managerial population agrees that in the conflict management process that promotes and effectively handles the situation with heart and brain, there is always a scope for a revaluation of interests and a revaluation of desires leading to a realignment of groups thereby retransformation of conflict potentialities adding plus values to the zero sum game that otherwise opted out in olden days.

6.3 Managing Conglomerated Conflict Behavioural Patterns

Most of the participants of the study indicated managing conflict behaviour as an individual's intended or displayed outward reaction to the conflict issue experienced. When a manager combines several kinds of behaviours when handling a disagreement with an opponent and such a handling mechanism is termed as conglomerated conflict behaviour, refers to a simultaneous or sequential aggregation of several behavioural components in varying degrees-in essence the root of the theory of conglomerate conflict behaviour. The theory of conglomerate conflict behaviour is more complex than other models and taxonomies based on Blake and Mouton's (1970) conflict management grid. Most theorists in this tradition use dual concerns (for example concern for own and other's goals), to determine the different behaviours or styles. However, the behavioural styles resulting from these concerns are usually presented as unique and independent, as if a person/manager uses only one 'conflict mode', for example competing. Also, the effects of these modes are typically reported separately for each mode, without considering possible covariating effects

(Huismans, 1995). The theory of conglomerate conflict states that the components of conflict behaviour should be considered as interrelated. That is, mixed motives result not in simple, but in complex behaviour, that is best analysed as a mixture of components. Interpersonal conflicts really are complex situations, in which different motives and concerns about own goals, the relation with the other, others' goals, as well as short and long-term objectives, direct behaviour.

The main reason why managers actually combine different styles, instead of using one single mode, seems that conflict situations are often mixed motive situations. According to many managers, they try to achieve personal outcomes, and try to reach a mutual agreement at the same time- typically combining cooperative and competitive behaviours. Critical for conflict behaviour is how managers think their goals are predominantly linked; these perceptions influence their expectations and actions, and thereby the outcomes of the conflict management. The importance of (perceived) interdependence on conflict behaviour is at the core of conglomeration of conflict behaviour.

As managers perceive more (positive) dependent relations, they agreed that they tend to behave primarily/predominantly cooperative, whereas competitive behaviour is elicited when the relation is experienced as independent or negatively related. These points to the unwritten rule that a conglomerate with relatively more competitive behaviour is related with less perceived interdependency, whereas a conglomerate with relatively more cooperative behaviour is related with a perceived greater interdependence between the parties (be it fellow managers/others). The two different conglomerates that are usually interpreted in contrast with one another, as a more cooperative and a more competitive approach is best suits for the deep analysis to the present study. In a real scenario as expressed by them, the two conglomerates represented offers however mixtures of both, competitive and cooperative behaviours, in rather different forms, not only excluding one another but also combining or supplementing each other. Both conglomerate behaviours are characterised by a fairly low use of avoiding and accommodating and by a relative prevalence of collaborating and competing approaches to the conflict handling.

Effective conglomerates are those that involve a dominant combination of benevolent competing and collaborating styles as indicated by most of the respondents. The scenario requires a deep analysis of the more objective outcomes of conflict handling behaviour that is certainly a possible extension for future research in the present area of study. Therefore, perspectives of parties and of other sources of information are needed in greater accuracy to potentially predict the conflict behavioural dynamics. Further, analysing the interaction between the resulting patterns should help us to understand why certain conglomerates are less or more effective. At the same time, when analysing interaction between the patterns, one can observe the adaptation of one subject to the other party's behaviour. So far, the conglomerate behaviour is an overall description of behaviour. Differentiating in sequences, might shed richer light on the development of conflict behaviour. It is likely that the found/identified conglomerates and their effectiveness differ as a function of context variables, including organisational and occupational culture, the issues at stake, and the relations among parties. It was expressed by few experts who participated in panel sessions that the usefulness of conglomerate conflict behaviour as a way of analysing conflict handling in organisational context can even be attuned with the predominant behavioural pattern though variations can be a possible notion.

6.4 Interdisciplinary teams and Conflict management

Almost all the participants in various sessions agreed that interdisciplinary teams comprising specialists from different functional areas (majority being the members of the study group) have the potential for greater creativity in business organisations. It can be accrued through observation that interactional dynamism among the human workforce in the business organisations convincingly appreciates interdisciplinary teams, usually comprising several departmental elements. Middle level managers are inevitable in every respect to these teams and their actions and responses makes black or white in the success nodes. *"Interdisciplinary teams draw on a wide variety of expertise and divergent perspectives to facilitate the production of creative ideas that are above and beyond the inherent capability of individuals and functionally homogeneous teams"*, expressed by a senior executive of a business organisation. Interdisciplinary teams benefit from differences of opinion about the work being done and improve their decision quality as team members share and adopt each other's new perspectives. The experts are of the opinion that synthesis that emerges from resolving different opinions is generally superior to the individual perspectives themselves. However, it seems that in many cases, despite the diversity of expertise at their disposal, interdisciplinary teams do not necessarily produce creative work because team members do not always share their unique knowledge and perspective. Team members may fear damaging their reputation, appearing incompetent, or they may simply wish to avoid conflict, where conflict in teams is described as awareness by some or all of the members of differences, discrepancies, incompatible wishes, or irreconcilable desires.

This is particularly salient in interdisciplinary teams where pride in one's field or specialty area can lead to team members feeling a need to protect their own intellectual territory. Many respondents expressed that interdisciplinary teams to produce creative work, team members must actively voice their unique ideas without fear of encroaching on interpersonal relationships , even if it means being aggressive or stubborn in defending dissenting perspectives to bring about change and improvement.

Regarding the creativity and problem solving, many focus group participants and few expert panel members are of the opinion that when the team is focused on creativity, two key processes are necessary for team performance- divergent and convergent thinking. Divergent thinking occurs when individuals or teams expand the possibilities under consideration by thinking *out of the box*. From a problem solving and reaching common ground perspective, divergent thinking is important because creativity is most usefully applied to ill-defined tasks where the problem is often fuzzy such that both the solution and the path to solution are unknown at the outset. Alternatively, findings from brainstorming research suggest that functional diversity in itself does not guarantee the production of creative ideas. Open dialogues in interdisciplinary team may not always facilitate the generation of creative ideas simply because not all ideas are heard let alone be considered.   By and large, this can be explained by research demonstrating that more often than not, groups have a tendency to actively consider and discuss only information that is commonly shared across members. Functional diversity in interdisciplinary teams is an important resource for the generation of creative ideas, functional diversity in itself does not determine creativity. Instead, the ways in which group processes leverage the knowledge resources provided by functional diversity critically determines the extent to which the potential for creativity is realised in interdisciplinary teams. In most of the organisations studied, either functional creativity oscillates in favour of homogeneous receptivity among the group members or to the dominant creative response/proactive measures initiated by the *first member* of the team. In an effort to examine the cognitive processes underlying the generation of creative ideas, it was repeatedly found through observations and focus groups that individuals who were motivated to attend to a flow of ideas from others produced more creative ideas than individuals who were not presented any cognitive stimulation. It can be pointed out that the key to knowledge creation is not so much the result of merely sharing information (as common wisdom suggests) but the effective integration of information shared. And perhaps most importantly, a critical aspect of effective integration of shared information is the manner in which teams manage conflict.

Top level officials preferred to say that the type of conflict in interdisciplinary teams and how they manage it is critical to creativity. They further said that in order to manage conflict, team members must be able to distinguish between conflict that is task, relationship, or process focused / dominant. It was observed that teams perform better on collaborating /problem solving and complex tasks when moderate levels of task conflict–conflict driven by differences in opinions or perceptions of the task being performed, is accompanied by low levels of relationship conflict–conflict arises from personality differences, hostility, and annoyance between individuals.

Managers agreed that interdisciplinary teams are particularly at risk for confusing one type of conflict for another. It is observed that the differences in background experience and communication styles coupled with a lack of deep knowledge of teammates make members of interdisciplinary teams relatively more prone to the misattribution of conflict than members of homogeneous teams, (e.g., intradepartmental teams can be considered as homogeneous and tasks that coexist in the organisation with more than one department can be termed as interdisciplinary). Interestingly, in addition to the critical role that minority dissent plays in team creativity, emotions accompanying dissent may play an important role in facilitating creativity in teams as observed throughout the study modes. Interdisciplinary teams experiencing emotional conflict – i.e. conflict arising as a result of dissatisfaction and frustration with the group's state of affairs, are likely to interpret the conflict as an indication that team members remain discontent with whatever solution is at hand and thus persist in their creative efforts to change and improve the status quo.

Managers agreed that positive emotions dampen the possibility of dissent and unique perspectives are never brought up because positive emotion indicates that all is well and there is no need to "discover the problem". This may be a cause of leniency towards maintaining status quo among most of the interactive teams in the studied organisations. In contrast, the presence of emotional conflict in interdisciplinary teams signals a discontentment and dissatisfaction with the status quo and thus motivates members to bring up dissenting views based on their specialised perspectives, visualised by many participants. Further divergent perspectives and dissatisfaction with the status quo are necessary but not sufficient for creativity in interdisciplinary teams. It was accrued that only teams experiencing emotional conflict will become aware of the discontentment and subsequently reveal and actively champion dissenting views. Interdisciplinary teams experiencing positive emotions can even be blissfully ignorant of potentially helpful divergent perspectives because discontentment and dissatisfaction never surface and it can be ascertained that the emotional conflict has a significant effect on creativity and the necessary appropriation of the conflict handling mechanism and the basic approach towards conflict management in organisations in general and teams in particular.

6.5 Conflict management and maximising helpful acts

A continuing question in the study of conflict and conflict management is, *"When is conflict helpful, and when it is harmful?"* Most of the focus group participants agree that conceptualising conflict as *simultaneously* containing helpful (conscious broadening and learning) and harmful (negative sentiment related) components in a way would be a right manner to critically analyse the dynamics of conflict management. Participants indicated that both conscious broadening and negative emotion can inhibit or promote future conflict, constituting feedback loops and this implies for conflict over time in terms of the efficacy of collaboration between parties who experience conflict. Traditionally *helpful* conflict has been called task conflict or cognitive conflict, while the *harmful* type of conflict is relationship or emotional conflict. Amidst managerial workforce, task conflict is centered on the group's objectives, or what it should do to solve a problem. It can be animated, but it is not personal. Relationship conflict is personal and emotional and tends to be about clashes of the members of the group. Task conflict, theorised to be positive is found to be negative in many cases of data accrual. Relationship conflict is seen as always negative, but in more humanised fields that deal with the stability of continuing relationships, relationship conflict can sometimes be helpful. It can be ascertained that functional and dysfunctional conflict perception seems to be a high influential factor among the managerial workforce.

Conflict, in addition to bringing about information, is usually experienced as somewhat unpleasant by the managers, and that this will lead to a buildup in negative feelings that over time; can prime people for more conflict. The first link in this had expressed by the expert panel sessions that- when people experience the unpleasantness of conflict, it can build up negative feelings. According to the managers, this happens in relationship conflict where people's personalities are attacked. This is an unpleasant experience that can evoke anger, irritation or annoyance and there may be other negative feelings that build as the result of conflict and to be managed appropriately. When conflict handling is avoided or delayed by protracted difficulties, this can be a frustrating experience. Here it is the inability to get to a reasonable state of affairs rather than anything personal that evokes the unpleasantness, and the particular feeling is one of frustration. In the case of a less powerful person trying to actively manage an important issue; it may be despair rather than frustration that emerges. Further managers opined that some negative feelings may be individual based. A person who simply is conflict avoidant may just experience displeasure as he or she is engaged in the conflict, even a relatively mild one. A person in a high status position may feel affronted that he or she is challenged by a lower status one. Across situations, people, and conflict types the mix of specific negative feelings may change, but in all cases the conflict itself is experienced as unpleasant to some degree, and leaves an emotional residue of feelings that are on the negative side of the continuum. When negative feelings build up, it should increase the likelihood of conflict. There are a number of ways in which negative feelings can provoke conflict. A very simple one is frustration-aggression and frustration has been shown to perpetuate the conflict cycles to come, agreed by most of the participants.

Another is reciprocity, where people who are experiencing something unpleasant can seek to return the unpleasantness in kind, especially if they feel justified. This follows an immediate downfall of ethical heights in the organisation in general and individual relationships in particular. Further, negative emotions crowds out cognitive capacity for other learning and active listening faculties of the parties of conflict. At the same time, emotion can lead one to either selectively attend or encode particular details, thus not comprehending the full story, but only the affect congruent parts (which would be objectively negative to the organisational learning).

Managers agree that all things put aside, with each conflict event; there is some increase in their *conscious expansion* regarding occupational dynamics, and some increase in negative and basically frustrating feelings. If there are more negative feelings than positive expansion of their consciousness, then the information brought about by the conflict event will go unused as people will not learn from each other. This effectively leaves frustration and conflict to spiral unabated as there is no learning to put the brakes on the *conflict-negative feelings spirals*. On the other hand, if conscious development outstrips negative emotion, there will be less conflict, and the unpleasantness of whatever conflict comes up should be overshadowed by the customisation that takes place. Thus there are fewer chances for conflict to produce unpleasantness, and the buildup of negative feelings will be diminished. If too much negative feelings exist among the group members, the scenario usually becomes unpleasant that no one will want to continue in the group and group effectiveness got reduced.

Some of the experts in the management field had revealed that some groups will seek to minimise all conflict and negative feelings. This kind of overzealous desire to have group harmony can be accomplished by inculcating people into the same way of thinking. In this scenario, any conflict would be an occasion for people to learn how to react to each other so that they avoid conflict in the future. The outcome here is groupthink. This was further strengthened and established through focus group, though seldom it occurs perpetually with the frequency it requires in the organisations brings a fact revealed. It can be attributed to the over conscious/cautious zeal among the managers to disassociate themselves from the middle path of compromise that may bring the memoirs of old day continuous streams of wanted and unwanted compromises they were forced to adopt to maintain all the group members equally satisfied.

The right balance in the minds of managers and their coworkers points the optimal situation where the conscious expansion and learning occurs at a high enough rates to control but not eliminate frustration, bringing a general satisfaction to the needy human elements in the organisation. This intuition is consistent with the multi level findings that trust can help increase the usefulness of task conflict, as trust should reduce the unpleasantness of conflict. It echoed in the sentimental expressions of many managers and their immediate occupational participants that people who trust each other may not make negative attributions about the conflict and makes the negativity to a more positive frame of reference adding plus values to the conflict management mechanism. At the practical level, a series of detailed and in-depth research needs to be done on how to find the balance between positive and negative outfits of the conflict management practices.

6.6 Culture, Emotion and Conflict management

Focus group sessions and expert panel inputs are lenient towards the new perspective on how organisational culture can shape beliefs about conflict, so much so that it renders them inconsistent with one of the most robust findings in conflict research and with what may appear to be common sense to other organisational/group cultures. One potential downside of the documented conflict literature in business organisations indicates that the groups containing relationship conflict are automatically handicapped from reaching their full potential. Managers who believe this may refrain from putting together the most qualified team because some interpersonal tension exists between particular individuals. Although the observation findings would not argue that such thinking is imprudent, they do suggest that it is also important to consider what the members think about conflict.

Top level officials stated that if all members who are otherwise parties to conflict agree that relationship conflict does not matter, then perhaps the way in which they interact will turn the beliefs into a self-fulfilling prophecy. From a practical standpoint, different individuals may hold different views about the relationship between conflict and performance and that both may be correct. The more organisation can help all group members be aware of each other's points of view, the better the group can become at knowing when to take advantage of opportunities that on first glance appear doomed and when to stay away from situations that look promising but would ultimately end in disaster.

Most of the sessions indicated that conflicts especially arising out of cultural differences can ofcourse disrupt trusting relationships as well as promote them. Family owned business organisations, being a forerunner in industrialisation had established synergistic yet traditionally bound organisational culture and the study group seems to be sustainer of the same. Recalling a conflict, managers quite often talk regretfully about losing their tempers or losing their heads and attribute the conflict factor to broader term—*cultural differences*. These colourful phrases aptly characterise the presumed differences that when people are in the middle of a conflict, they behave emotionally often because of the differences exists beyond the occupational understanding. When they discount the influence of emotional factors, they are likely to fail to plan for how they will handle their emotions. This tendency has implications for how managers will respond when they find themselves embroiled in interpersonal conflicts especially the responses they may receive from the other end. An interesting observation was accrued which echoes the pragmatic treatment of this issue. In this case, a manager intends to have a calm discussion with his fellow worker about organisational chores. Beforehand, he knows that he should try to stay calm if he wants to identify a constructive solution to the problem. However, the discussion quickly takes a turn, tempers flare, and an argument ensues.

It was observed that though the manager had every intention of discussing the situation in a reasonable way, he underestimated the degree to which either he or his colleague would react emotionally. In retrospect, the manager regrets having had the argument and believes that they should have talked about the problem more calmly in an effort to identify a solution. Most of the managerial participants agreed that whether thinking ahead to an anticipated conflict or thinking back on a past conflict, emotional reactions will be less prominent than they will be at the time of the conflict. Further individuals' reactions will be more emotional when they are picturing themselves in the middle of conflict than when they are either looking back on a conflict or looking ahead to an anticipated conflict. "Confronted with interpersonal conflicts, it appears that people follow their gut reactions and fail to act in their best long-term interests", expressed by atleast three managers. Managers seem to follow their *hearts* when they respond to conflict to a greater degree than they follow their *heads*. This is especially true when they are in the middle of a conflict. This means that managers who anticipate an interpersonal conflict–particularly when they are thinking about what they want to do in that situation need to be aware that tempers may flare in the heat of the argument. This response is likely to come at the expense of a more thoughtful, rational response, and it may lead to a poor outcome. Moreover, these hot-headed reactions are likely to be the very kind that produces regret, especially in the short-term and continuously affects the relationship or task at hand. Many subordinates of the managerial population indicated that the emotions provide useful signaling information about the importance of the dispute or the significance of the relationship but flaring tempers can easily fuel the conflict and diminish the likelihood of finding a reasonable solution.

Even if parties are able to continue their dialogue, the emotionality of their interaction is likely to prevent them from thinking creatively about potential mutually beneficial solutions. However, that it is negative emotionality that creates the greatest risks to collaborative conflict handling. Positive affect, on the other hand, is associated with cognition and behaviour that increases the likelihood those parties will realise mutually beneficial outcomes, both at the short and long run. Anger or other negative emotions interfere with the ability to manage the conflict effectively; managers may need to plan even more carefully for the interaction. To ensure that cooler heads prevail, managers may need to take steps to limit the emotionality of their responses. They might consider dealing with the other person in a setting in which emotional outbursts would be inappropriate, for instance. Although they cannot predict what the other party may do, they would be wise to consider what the other party might want to do in the heat of the argument influenced by the organisational culture and individual emotions.

6.7 Building bridges or be at doldrums

"Never ever remain a middle manager in this business; it's the fastest way to spoil you, before your time and energy counts", remarked a factory manager. Nearly a decade ago management thinkers all over the world talked of three factors that effectively motivate middle-level managers. These were–trust, respect and caring, which they stated were an integral part of well-run, successful companies.

Today, most business organisations studied under this academic query are keen on modernising their strategies to improve employee morale and productivity. But the amount of effort people are willing to put in depends on the degree to which their motivational needs are met. And they have a long way to go as far as trust and respect go. Irrespective of who forms the guidelines and sets the goals it still falls on the middle managers to see that they are successfully implemented. This is because they are in the unique position in the organisations to see and review what works and what doesn't and if doesn't what changes could be made to see that it does. It was observed and accepted by various sessions that in many units, middle managers are not expected to make executive decisions. Their authority as well as responsibility level is perceived to be low hence they are quite content, being where they are as long as they can pass the work to someone up. However in a few organisations, it's the other way around. Here, the top management is not aware of the day-to-day operations and rely on the middle managers. When things do not go according to plan rather than admit to faulty planning, the middle managers are fired. But despite their hands on experience, most often, the top management pays scant attention to the suggestions or ideas from middle level managers.

They may give a patient ear to his suggestions but as far as implementation of ideas goes the middle manager has to toe the top managerial line. It is frustrating surely when the top management expects middle managers to implement reforms but neither supports their efforts nor acknowledges it. So, what can a middle manager do in this situation? When he knows that it is he who knows his people, he who has the ideas that are workable but his own bosses don't care a howl.

Some of the managers indicated that they can go on doing what they have always done and not care. They forget/forced to forget about making a contribution to the organisation, if they are content to get their pay cheque on time every month, this aspect shouldn't pose too much of a problem in many cases. But, if some manager happens to be one who cares, he had to work out for others and the only way to start is to initiate a dialogue with top management and tell them as it is. It seems that this step could be usually misconstrued by top executives and could be detrimental to the career of middle managers. Perhaps middle level managers may find a pair of friendly ears willing to listen and if they can find a champion for the cause of the organisation, half the battle is won- a fact repeated very often by many managers and their subordinates in various sessions. If not, they have to decide about the repercussions that are going to be bad and a contingency plan.

An important point to remember is that managers don't criticise any plans or actions that they have been asked to implement without having a very good reason as to why they may not work, reinstated by almost all the participants including top level executives. If possible, middle level managers may ask for permission to try out a course of action that they think may work, supplementing past, successful and related attempts. However, managers indicated that they should take every steps to shield themselves be branded as between taking initiative and insubordination. It was observed that, to deliberately disregard a top manager's directive will not be viewed as courageous but as indisciplinary. Whether a person decide to speak up or not if he had decided that enough is enough, should consider all the social, economical, private, and other related issues. There seems that it is indeed thankless and frustrating to be the middle person/ manager— an organisational sandwich between the top management and the bottom-rung employees; painting it as *black* or a *white paper revelation* or still as a *grey mattered one*. But it projections indicated that despite all these constraints or perceived notations, there is a constant and lively expansion among the middle managerial cadre in business organisations. A senior manager expressed as that *"...we are termed as middle level managers because... we are necessarily in the middle and we may be shifted to top or bottom without consulting the middle portion (I mean heart), and I may not be correct if I add   the word 'Unceremoniously' to the above"*, explains tonnes of thoughts that are usually behind every conflict managerial practice exercised by middle level manager.

The psychological dimensions of conflict management was repeatedly emphasised by the focus group participants. In case of in- depth interviews, many managers had indicated that there exists a greater need to see the conflict and conflict management from collectivistic and psychological perspectives. They further indicated that there exists the unificatory power of conflict memory which makes the conflict transactions in an organisational life possible. This necessitates to consider all conflict sequences - not just of an individual- is taken to rest on the foundation of a single subjective knower/wisher/doer who playfully proliferates himself into this ephemeral show of fragmentation and then connection, experience and then recall, forgetting and then re-discovery of his own identity.

Through the content analysis of organisational documents as well as the psychological literature concerning self psychology, it can be inferred that conflict perception or direct experience of conflict situations seems to be one thing and remembering and managing it quite something else. Conflict perception of a currently available object of concern or even an introspective enjoyment of a reflexive cognitive or affective state seems to be quite easily separable from conflict memory which is supposed to be concerned with the past and the absent. But this first impression is deceptive. A kind of short term immediate sensory memory through the triggering event is essential for any conflict perception to happen. For perceptual conflict, however instantaneous it may appear, occupies a depth of duration, the illusion of simultaneity being created by rapid successions like a needle going through hundred lotus petals as if at the same time and underlying current of all this is in incalculable multiplicity of conflict memories which are past and absent.

The synthetic functions of cognition, selection, attention, recognition, judgement, hedonic and evaluative assessment are all dependent upon some form of stringing together of individualistic conflict strings in conflict fabric experiences across time and recalling the previous ones. And of course inference, the use of language and other conscious human practices require active use of conflict memory. Even the phenomenal qualia or subjective 'what it is like to be' character of a process of conflict consciousness requires that it feels a certain way for undergo it. And without some narrative implicit episodic conflict memory or atleast recognitional capacity one would not even have a sense of being one self managing conflict.

Expert panel sessions had revealed that in cases of managing the organisational conflicts, conflict recognition and conflict memory need not be bracketed together; since conflict recognition falls under perceptual re-identification of what is currently presented to the senses. Conflict memory is a fresh experience; whereas recollection- which is the chief meaning of conflict memory is always of what is absent and past.

Conflict consciousness intimately involves conflict memory of some form or other. The sense of self, self-continuation and the self-other distinction throughout the conflict managerial plane should be a prerequisite in this regard. The sense of past and hence the awareness of any duration at all should be a strengthening agent to this module. Further the ability to recognise and reidentify objects and other similar and dissimilar entities, ability to form concepts, linguistic capacity, rule following patterns and other emotive denominations including its expressions are all needed to propel conflict consciousness which is of different plane from memory and perception. Managing conflicts needs to focus on expanding the conflict consciousness and strengthening thereby the facets of conflict perception, conflict memory and its denominations. Not just language as a carrier of this expressive domains but all the non verbal cues in particular and any rational practice which involves inference or application of general rules requires that ability to link back with past experiences, their objects and most importantly the ability to synthesise a successive series of experiences under a single unified cognising integral and integrative conflict management-a transcendental unity of apperception must be capable of accompanying all cognitive acts. The essential role played by this linking back or connecting after principles, subjective synthesis can be done by the power of conflict memory.

Many managers indicated that such common day to day practices such as establishing cause-effect relationships, remembering and exposure of error in a previous piece of awareness require a single knower as their foundations. Further it was observed that even all minor popular not so pure activities such as unitary social intercourses and assumptive pure activities like collaborative transformations are possible on the basis of unity of a cogniser. Thus all practices simply live on synthesis. This prepares the organisational entities for a greater creative learning which transcends Pavlovian conditioning, Skinners operants, vicarious learning and even the clean slate theories of learning. *Amygdala*-the currently recognised brain area responsible for emotional reactions and the platform for selective attention are all seems to be building blocks of the greater secrets of conflict managerial understanding and the learning to manage is yet to be unlocked.

7.1 Conflict management strings (CMS/SPT Model)

An attempt was made to postulate a model in this regard with the data accrued through expert panel interviews as well as the content analysis of available conflict literature along the psychological plane. In a typical organisational context, conflict sequences and its responses - not just of an individual can be visualised with the advent of prenotions of the strings of conflict management   which are of unimaginably microcosmic, illusionary yet dynamic packets of energies of managing conflicts. Bionic, psycho-physic-enviro principles, cosmic laws and other quantamised nature of conflict and its management may be attempted to explain with these conflict strings. though it seems to follow a different language of its own.

Infinitively small dissonance- resonance self balance of past and future experienced by a bio-psycho-social microcosmic entity in a time and space influenced by the factors of social, economic, political, technical, industrial, cultural, legal and ecological in origin can be referred as a *conflict management string or SangharshaPrabandhaTantri*- SPT (in Sanskrit this means - strings of conflict management). It necessarily rejects the mechanistic orders of traditional conflict resolution and or managerial approaches. The key features of the SPT model that creatively replaces some of the illustrious decelerating notions of past are thus follows-

- The conflicts experienced in mind-intelligence-consciousness of managers are out of operative conflict management strings-SPT normally in zillions than the pure singular entity causal relationship explored in the past. An SPT can be compared to a small tree in the earth whereas the unitary emotional expression of a social entity to the size of the solar system. This supplements the theories of multiple conflict notions by different managers who are in same organisational set up and calls for integral conflict management which revolves around life principle management.

- The movements of SPTs are in general discontinuous in the sense that action is constituted of indivisible dissonance –resonance balance and its influentials implying that it can go from one state to another, without passing through any states in between. This clarifies the dynamism of conflicts and their strange appearance-disappearance. The helical, spiral, non directional, multidimensional and other conflict movement and mapping can be better explained with this postulation.

- SPTs can show different properties, depending on the environmental context within which they exist and are subject to observation and apperception. This may explain the extrageneous influence and its importance in case of conflict management issues among the managers.

- Conflict management strings-SPTs are peculiar entities which can be called as living from a different sense of its meaning as they self balance, yet they are of non living as a unitary conceptual frame of operation. They are part of greater conflict fabric which is certainly universalistic and single conscious, one without a second in every organisational levels-thus influencing managerial understanding of conflicts and its management.

- Two or more SPTs which initially combine to form a conflict bit, may show a peculiar non local relationship which can best be described as a non-causal connection of elements of conflicts that are far apart. Multiple and multitudinal effects of conflict sources and its management can be explained with this postulation.

- If all human notions are of discrete SPTs, the interactions between different SPTs constitute a single structure of indivisible links, so that the entire conflict has to be thought of as an unbroken whole, each element of conflict that managers can abstract in thought shows basic properties that depend on its overall environment. This in a way is much more reminiscent of how the organs constituting living beings are related, than it is of how parts of a machine interact. In essence organismic nature of conflict is to be adhered so as to manage it. Managers collective mind and their belongingness can be compared as such an incorporated conflict consciousness spectrum which employs tangible and other modes of operations thereby finding a greater amass of synergy in managing conflicts.

- SPTs are self evolving, self managing, metamorphosing, constructively multitudinal, and part of a greater organisational as well as social fabric which can be referred as Mother SPT (MSPT). SPTs are also logically possible to be included in organisational resource-both living and non- living domains too. SPTs create, nourish, sustain and dissemble themselves at their own principles and calls for integrated management of the same for attaining organisational goals by the managers.

SPTs are temporarily permanent and permanently temporary too all at the same time but not at the space dimensions. SPTs breeds and effectualise parallel SPTs which are tuned to different dissonance- resonance balances, not necessarily be in same time and space. This can be explained with the changing and dynamic nature of conflicts and its various dimensions. Furthermore it necessitates conscious managerial interventions for integrated conflict management.

SPTs may exist even in supra cortex consciousness or the fourth state of consciousness and all the intuitive conflict management can be attributed to this. Managers do agree that they do take intuitive decisions while managing conflicts.

Individual SPTs are deemed to be influenced by karmic (ancient Indian theory of *multi cause-multitudinal*) principles of interconnectivity, integration, multidimensional projection and super positioning and such field is visualised as an energy field which transcends the time and space in its most observational unitarian denominations yet unattached to this in its SPT fabric. This in turn calls for integral conflict management approaches for managers along the lines of life principles studded with ethical and moral dimensions in organisational life.

It can be observed and can be postulated that SPTs are managing the dissonance-resonance through various proactive interventions. One among them can be regarded as the ancient Indian politico-ethical methodology of Sama-Dana-Bheda-Danda-Maya-Upeksha-Indrajala domiciles. *Sama* denotes that which brings equipoise or tranquility to the consciousness. It is the art of gentle persuasion and revolves around the conciliatory approach. *Dana* means the usage of giving something in return to achieve managerial purpose and can be denoted as bestowing approach of modern managerial understanding of *carrot and stick. Bheda* is the art of aggravating dissension amongst elements opposed to each other and means to create discrimination, make a difference, intentionally creating a gap by following oxymoron. This seems to be similar with the *divide and govern policy* in modern times. If social unit is insensitive even to the difference, then *Danda,* the punishment and or creative destructions happen. *Maya* means the use of managerial illusions or deceit. It seems to be deceptive to the core. *Upeksha* is to deliberately ignore influentials so as to achieve unitary purpose and follows the principles of modern day *active avoidance. Indrajala* literally means jugglery and intend for balancing acts amongst opposing pulls. *Indrajala* brings false manipulations to the conflict situations. Managing dissonance-resonance with this approach can bring integrated conflict management which can creatively deal the conflict situations. This in turn helps to enhance constructive conflict management mechanisms among the managers.

- SPTs have inbuilt and creative tendencies for win-win approaches as well as zero sum games as they make interactions between or amongst themselves. This indicates that effective conflict management requires much more than the use of specific techniques. The ability to understand and correctly diagnose conflict is essential to managing it. Expert panel reviews had indicated that managers are required to understand the conflicts and after diagnosing the same may take necessary steps for managing the conflicts.

- Executives in the organisations indicated that conflict management domains are yet to be subjected to laboratory verifications. Constructive conflict management auras, more and more humane as well as intuitive conflict management are some of the possible resultants of well balanced zillions of SPTs. They are omni present in the unitary social intercourse-be it from intra-individualistic, interpersonal or even organisation wide happenings. It recalls the idea that constructive conflict management requires organisation (systems)-wide understanding and managing the conflicts through systematic efforts.

Managers are of the opinion that application of conflict management techniques will highly depend on the nature and causes of conflicts in the organisation. Kottler had rightly observed that conflict management even consists of diagnostic processes, interpersonal styles, negotiating strategies and other interventions that are designed to avoid unnecessary conflicts and reduce or resolve excessive conflict. Furthermore if the conflict is not dysfunctional but it is leading to healthy competition, it can even be encouraged. However, it is unlikely that a conflict is constructive in the absence of proper organisational climate. A major part of organisational climate as relevant to conflict management is built through common goals and proper structural arrangement. This paves way and further necessitates exploring integral and other integrative approaches of managing conflicts. In this regard, above explained SPT model can help a lot to understand the integrative dynamics of conflict management.

7.2 Aura of Conflict Management

According to some expert panel reviews, conflict management approaches can be considered as a conglomeration and multitudinal situational-responses exercised by the parties of conflict. This idea seems to be getting strengthened by systematic observation carried out by the researcher in selected business units. The spectrum of managerial options in cases related with conflicts reinforces the multiple preferential mechanisms. This imbibes a culture of extendable and or a combination of under mentioned managerial approaches broadly identified through this study. The managerial understanding about organisational conflicts needs to be rejuvenated so as to mirror the field reality. Many executives and some experts are of the opinion that the definition of theoretical conflict management, when viewed through the prisms of organisational realities needs to be embedded with veracity and requires refurbishment to the futuristic needs. It can be accrued that conflict management shall refer to all conscious and or unconscious dynamic interventions that enable to promote a sustainable conflict intensity level which stems out of transitional and or transformational process at a given setting. An attempt was made in this regard to define the resultant oriented approaches of conflict management with renewed and more reflective perspectives.

- **Conflict Prevention** - Conflict prevention shall refer to all result oriented strategies for achieving sustainable retrogradation and/or putting an end to the status quo.
- **Conflict Stimulation-** Conflict stimulation refers to those conscious facilitations by accelerating the intensity level of conflict among the target elements.
- **Conflict Mitigation-** Conflict mitigation refers to all balancing and transitional interventions, creating circumstances permitting greater leniency to the net conflict intensity.
- **Conflict Regulation-** Conflict regulation shall refer to all authoritative reconciliatory strategies which direct the conflict energy to the 'right path'.
- **Conflict Resolution-** Conflict resolution refer to all process oriented activities that aim to address the underlying causes of direct, cultural and structural incompatibility and wishes to reframe the conflict as a shared problem with mutually acceptable solutions. It envisages how parties can move from zero-sum game/destructive patterns to positive-sum constructive outcomes.
- **Conflict Resonance-** Conflict resonance shall refer to all dynamic reinforcement or prolongation of constructive conflict harmony thus synchronised by conflict stakeholders and other organisational elements.
- **Conflict Transformation-** Conflict transformation is a continuous process of engaging with and transforming the relationships, interests, transactions and if

necessary, the very constitution of destructive conflictual practices. It must actively envision, include, respect and promote the human and cultural resources from within a given setting. This involves a new set of our understanding through which we do not often see the setting and the people in it as the problem and our solutions as the sole answer. Rather, we understand the long term goal of transformatary values as validating and building on people and resources within a given setting.

Probably the concept of conflict management is broad enough to include manifold and realistic situational responses- be it constructive, creatively destructive, cultural, and synthesised or conflict-stakeholder specific. These are certainly to be differentiated from the cosy nostrums of constructive/destructive brandishing conflict management. Furthermore, organisational life and conflicts are intertwined more in these days than ever before. From identifying the positive sparks of the organisational life to the evaluation of the law of karma (Indian concept of *causal - effect*), every elemental influence enshrine with its weightages when deciding managerial conflicts and its channelisation process. Distributive elements of conflict management among the studied population indicate a collection of patterns and selective/integral ones are modelised under the umbrella concept of conflict management. In a more realistic situation it may not be possible to manage all conflicts experienced by the managers from a mere humanistic bio-psycho-social plane of operations. Higher angel touches are needed which propel the management to more transcendental heights and the heightened conscious will make conflict management. This may sound a close call to spiritualistic side of conflict management. The concepts of self-actualisation (popularised by Abraham Maslow) and Karmic (cause-effect) theories of Indian psyche are all nothing but various shades of principled life style and conscious conflict management. According to some executives, this can be referred as supra conscious conflict management. Interestingly an addendum to supra conscious conflict management is also possible acting diagrammatically opposite to it which can be termed as conflict oppression. The supra conscious conflict management being an active tracker of conflict management- excels in dynamism, varieties and creative solutions. Conflict oppression is essentially an assortment of managing conflicts by destruction and even includes active avoidance. It ranges from simple destruction of a conflict to creative and synthesised destructions. Organisational life situations channelise the resultant oriented conflict management approaches and present itself as a cyclic phenomenon throughout the conflict management frame.

Most of the managers are not really thinking about how they approach conflict. It just happens to them and they do have their preferential domains, normally to avoid the conflicts. When conflict arises, managers agree that they tend to play out their roles like scripts based on their behavioural and conflict management styles. Effective conflict management can only be achieved when a manager begins to really see how her or his conflict management style is actually self-destructive. Managers are required to get exposure in the contemporary conflict management philosophy; especially along the lines of interactionist, integral and integrated ones. Emotional immaturity seems to at its worst during conflict situations as expressed by the managers. In order to change, managers have to *want* to change. Interestingly managers had expressed and the same was revealed by the findings that they want to change and equip themselves with the skills of conflict management. These indicate the need to impart training with an exclusive focus on conflict management skill enhancement among the business managers. Guided conflict management modules for business managers can be a better suggestive measure and the same is expressed in tabular form in the following section. Further the critical factors to be considered for imparting conflict management training were identified and put forth as suggestive measures.

8.1 Modules of conflict management training

Effective conflict management is situational. That is, managers must be trained to apply emotional intelligence to deal with each person and situation differently. Conflict management training sessions should be designed the same way. It must include all the right elements to really reach the managers, including humour, role play, direct confrontation, facilitated discussions, exercises and group activities besides the skill sets that are vital for endorsement.

Conflicts are often characterised by considerable social complexity, managing these processes often call for much effort to build rapport for stakeholder engagement, facilitate negotiations, carefully prepared agreements and assistance in the implementation or monitoring of such agreements. Addressing conflicts can be therefore extremely time-consuming, and emotionally draining. Individual organisations in their own capacities require substantial resources for meetings, transport, materials and other logistics. To increase the chances that such processes are sustained, it is worthwhile developing a participant selection process that identifies participants who are already helping parties in organisational conflicts at various levels and have facilitation and field-based experience in conflict management. Ideally, the training group includes participants who are already linked to conflictual parties' social networks and have credibility with the parties or people in authority who can provide assistance. This necessitates not only the water tight managerial group but also transgresses the hierarchical levels. Such a commitment can only occur over an extended period if conflict management is visualised as a priority for the trainee's organisation. An integrated and visionary approach in this regard is guidelined below.

Table 8.1 Contents, objectives and methodology on imparting conflict management skill set

Module Contents	Sub contents	Specific objectives	Training Methodology
1) Concept and sources of conflict 2) Concept of Constructive conflict management 3) Methods of conflict handling and conflict management styles 4) Institutionalised mechanism for conflict management among individual companies, government, associative and legalistic levels 5) Various approaches for conflict management-Integral, Interactionist and Integrated 6) Leadership development on problem-solving, development-oriented attitude and social communication skills 7) Negotiating and active listening skills 8) Counselling skills 9) Assessing Conflict management skills 10) Culture, Consensus and Conflict management 11) Emerging conflict management models	a) Conflict Analysis b) Stakeholder Analysis c) Conflict and early response d) Proactive conflict management e) Gender sensitivity f) Organisational Change and Developmental factors g) Factors of Transformational leadership h) Interpersonal effectiveness and human relations' approach i) Psychometric skills j) SPT model for conflict management	▪ To identify the sources of conflict ▪ To clarify the concepts of conflict and Constructive conflict management ▪ To understand the process of effective conflict management ▪ To plan collaboration with all stakeholders for Win-Win ▪ To clarify the institutional set-up and interests of stakeholders in conflict-management ▪ To identify various approaches of conflict management ▪ To understand the principles of transformational leadership ▪ To uplift essential skill sets of conflict management	▪ Lecture-cum-discussion ▪ Role-playing ▪ Brainstorming ▪ Self-analysis techniques ▪ Simulation games ▪ Field visit to success and failure sites ▪ Story telling and problem-solving ▪ Case study ▪ Group-analysis techniques

8.2 Critical factors to be considered while imparting conflict management training

Multiple and integrated phased training programmes shall be appropriate and effective for skill building on conflict management. Further, the combination of classroom training and mentor-supported field practice can be explored and the same will result in effective learning through practice and increased appreciation of the relevance of conflict management to managers' job responsibilities. Wider participatory group incorporating executives, supervisors, workers etc can be explored in future training sessions. Long term effectiveness of skill building training programmes for conflict management depends on a number of critical factors. These include first and foremost careful selection of participants as well as provision for ongoing support for conflict management processes by business organisations. Some of the critical factors to be considered while imparting conflict management training are explained below-

- Conflict management training sessions will be more effective when it is directed to a group of affiliated people, rather than to individuals. The training of individuals often results in the random application of skills. A cadre of two or more people, however, can work together to mutually support each other in the development of strategies for managing conflicts. Departmental and other stratification can be explored in this case.
- Conflict management training may ideally target the managers and other staff together, so that they can coordinate their conflict management activities.
- Conflict management training a small group of people in a small geographic area effectively will be better than training a larger group in a wider area where lack of resources, isolation or inability to impart training modules will reduce the training's effectiveness.
- It will be more effective to train a group of people working in a single company/ organisation as this promotes the institutionalisation of procedures.
- Skill-building trainings need to be well integrated in participants' organisations to ensure that participants enjoy the required organisational support for their work.
- New intermediaries in a conflict need support, encouragement and strategy assistance. As an integral part of training, it will certainly be useful to provide periodic mentoring/coaching - via e-mail, telephone and most importantly through field visits and active interaction with the parties of conflict, wherever feasible. Suitable local training institutions should be involved in training and post-training mentoring from the outset, to build local capacity for the replication of training

9.1 Managerial essentials for conflict management

- The manager has to address himself to what is important to people from their point of view as well as from his own and make sure he does not confuse the two.

- The manager has to address himself to people's feelings, attitudes and personal background as well as to their general logical motives and purposes.

- The manager has to look at the relationships people have with one another and make sure whether these relationships helps to attain more logical purposes of psycho-social bonding and contributes to the social bonding within the organisational sphere.

- The manager has to reflect himself as more than logical in theory and be creative at times.

- Functionally, the manager being a practitioner of the skills of diagnosis should be at home with the skills of communication and actions.

- A manager who is helping people to feel secure, to learn from their own experience, to reach their own decisions and to become more mature and independent is greatly appreciated by the organisational circles.

9.2 Creating plus values by skillful conflict management

The time is now ripe to think of a new whole philosophy of managing the conflicts in the organisation based upon individuals-his desires, instincts, habits and behaviour. In its true sense individual is not treated to be as an individual but as a member of the groups where the same habits and desires float up as in his personal life. True and positive managerial examination of human relationships as the bedrock of business organisations can alone bring the dynamic peace and the highly spoken plus value for the business organisations.

Managing conflict effectively requires many professional qualities and skills, and changing organisations to be conflict-positive, requires on-going, persistent actions. To become effectively and for appropriately managing conflict, middle level managers must understand the causes, theories, approaches and strategies of conflict management. This requires determining the kind of experiences in conflict management and its adequacy in preparing managers for conflict situations. The study indicates that the preparation in conflict management should start early and body of knowledge should be included along the professional socialisation process from the beginning of every managerial entry levels. It should include, in the first stage, the knowledge of the causes of conflicts, the conflict process and the skills required. Teaching problem-solving and decision-making approaches to cooperative conflict management adding plus values should be together in an integrated fashion. Managers/potential managers should; through planned exercises– be able to negotiate and analyse strategies and tactics for effectively implementing their available power in conflicts. Skill and comfort in using a variety of conflict-handling modes may help to develop a repertoire of conflict managerial skills that are essential in effectively managing the variety of conflict situations. Learning in the work environment can also be done through observations. Superiors may serve as role models. Role modeling can be an effective teaching learning strategy, providing upcoming managers have the skills and abilities required. In addition to the importance of education and skill training when conflict occurs in the unit, managers must deal appropriately with that conflict. Consistently using strategies with *Win–Lose* or *Lose– Lose* outcomes will create disharmony within the unit. The skills desired in enacting the facilitation role in handling intergroup conflict includes counselling, transparent and non violent communication, building better interpersonal relations and the ability for giving and receiving feedback on behaviour.

Only a small percentage of time is spent in true collaboration in the work environment among many business organisations, especially when there is a wide difference in power between individuals or groups involved. Managing effectively conflicts in a unit/department requires using strategies to actively encourage subordinates to attempt to handle their own problems, communicating honestly and openly, ensuring clarity of responsibility of roles, creating policies and changing if needed, and being sensitive to others and offer support.

In these days, managerial understanding is evolving itself through various phases of operations and a manager needs to understand in its most dynamic way the trends and quintessence of managerial appropriations. A word in this regard may help them; *they can't do it by themselves*, no matter how smart they are. Markets move too quickly, technologies grow too complex, and too many smart people are investing too much time and money in innovation. And, by the way, lots of those smart people are working in teams, trying to beat *them* out.

Grey areas of managerial understanding may only be surmounted by the fruits of experience. Managers are real persons with blood and beauty and they need the necessary exposure, expedition and experience to handle the intricacies of emerging scenario. One of the major challenge counted by practicing managers and other stakeholders of contemporary management ethos, is the expressive development of a body of theory to explain why organisational conflicts take the form they do, and why they/others behave as they do, including various stratum of the managerial responses towards conflict dynamics. Outlining some aspects of this emerging line of research on organisations and to call attention to a number of related methodological issues that play an important role in these areas of research – the relation between situational processes, handling strategies and theories, the importance to the research effort of the choice of tautologies and definitions, the nature of evidence, behavioural reengineering, process realignment, organisational preparedness/ adaptability/receptivity and the role of personality-structure interplays among other related domains, enshrine the expanding horizons. Something is *common knowledge* if it is known to each person, and in addition, each person knows that he or she has this knowledge; knows that the other person/s knows the person knows it; and so forth. If in any case, a crevice in this structure entitles a need to acquire the *savoir faire* and to transform the relationship to new heights. It exactly suits for the expanding domains of conflict management studies concerning managers, supervisors, executives and common workers in business organisations. The current study can be equated with a modest attempt to promote knowledge about conflict management and to share the intricacies of the practice of conflict management with a special emphasise on managerial modalities that brings forth a plethora of opportunities.

9.3 Interactionist approaches for better conflict management

The emerging view of conflict, called as interactionist view, reverses many of the cozy nostrums of human relations management in business organisations. The interactionist view of conflict has a broader scope than the traditional notions of unitary and pluralist perspectives which are in a way shy away to address the conflict at all. Interactionist view recognises that in some cases conflict may be helpful, facilitative and functional. The current thought acknowledges the inevitability of conflict and focuses it as a useful tool / vehicle to shake the organisation from stereo type / contention to innovation and creativity. One of the most outstanding aspects of organisational conflict is that it is practically intrinsic to the life and dynamics of organisations. Conflict seems to be present in interpersonal relations, in intragroup and intergroup relations, in strategic decision-making and other organisational episodes. As many authors have pointed out (De Dreu & Van de Vliert, 1997; Pondy, 1967) that conflict is a phenomenon that may give rise to both beneficial and functional consequences, as well as having important positive and negative effects on individuals, groups and organisations. Therefore, it is necessary to exercise managerial aura and to have access to diagnosis and intervention tools that may allow it to handle conflicts appropriately.

The object of conflict management is not the promotion of scientific investigation and discovery of managerial principles, but rather the assimilation and interpretation of that which has been or shall be hereafter discovered, and its application to organisational welfare, especially by the building of the truths of human relations and organisational philosophy into the structure of a broadened and purified management. Such a managerial understanding will greatly stimulate intelligent effort for the improvement of human conditions and the advancement of organisational development in strength and excellence of character. To this end, it is desired that an array of theories and postulates given by men and women in their respective departments – on managerial disciplines, psychology, sociology, ethics; all sciences and branches of knowledge which have an important bearing on the subject; all the great laws of nature, especially of evolution including organisational fruition. And also such interpretations as are in accord with the spirit of the organisation concerned, to the end that the human spirit may be nurtured in the fullest light of the world's knowledge and that organisational human being may be helped to attain their highest possible welfare and happiness upon this earth. The spectrum of conflict management in the business organisations requires an immediate attention. The buzz word of functional cooperation can be a reality if and only if the managerial decisions are supplemented by the facets of reciprocal relating, integrative unity, law of the situation and cumulative responsibility. A word for the managers-you are not only for what you said and did, but how you said and did it. And that's the quintessence of conflict management.

9.4 Emerging approaches of conflict management- integral and integrated

Modern researches and organisational studies speak of managing the conflicts, the evolution of conflict addressing in organisational life, but management is a word which merely states the situational responses without explaining it. For there seems to be no reason why conflict management should evolve out of material and other elements or mind management out of living form, unless the modern day management gurus explicitly accepts the integrating and all embracing dimensions of it. Modern organisational conflicts are a form of veiled organisational life, organisational life a form of veiled consciousness. And then there seems to be little objection to a farther step in the series and the admission that mental consciousness may itself be only a form and a veil of higher states which are beyond organisational citizenship. The significance of this organisational philosophy applied to the conflict management lies in the fact that it is not speculative in character but is rooted in the theory and practice of organisational conflict management and expounds in philosophical terms the results of the present study in the wider spectrum of organisational consciousness studies. To this the current organisational researchers must accept vestiges of non-computability to be present, at some indiscernible level, in inanimate manner.

An essential ingredient is missing from the present day conflict management picture. This missing ingredient would be needed in order that the central issues of humane approaches in organisations could ever be accommodated within a coherent conflict management world-view. It is a direction that involves an important change in the most basic of our organisational understanding. The resultants of this study are fairly specific about what the nature of the directional change must be and how it might apply to the management of conflicts. Even with the limited present understanding of the nature of conflict management and its missing ingredient, managers can begin to point to where it must be making its mark and how it should be providing one vital contribution to whatever it is that underlies our conscious feelings and actions of organisational life. The precision and scope of principles of management in general and the theories of conflict in particular as presently appreciated is extraordinary, yet they contain no hint of any action that cannot be simulated computationally. Nevertheless, within the possibilities that these management inputs allow us, we must try to find an opening for a hidden non computational action that the functioning of organisational conflict management must somehow be taking advantage of. The present study asserts that managers must look to the phenomenon of quantum scale reduction to see where our present picture of managerial reality must indeed be fundamentally changed. For management to be able to accommodate something that is as foreign to the current physical picture as is the phenomenon of conflict management, organisations must expect a profound change- one that alters the very underpinnings of the philosophical viewpoint as to the nature of organisational reality. For now, organisations may try to ask a somewhat simpler-sounding questions regarding where one might expect that conflict management is to be found in the known organisational world and worlds of common managers.

To obtain an understanding of the relationship of the sources of conflicts and management of the conflicts has, however thus far proved to be extremely difficult and this difficulty has its root in the very great difference in their basic qualities as they present themselves in the organisational experiences. This difference can be expressed with particularity, the sources of conflicts as 'extended substances' and the management of conflicts as 'thinking substances'. Evidently, by extended substances, organisations can infer that those are something made up of distinct forms existing in space, in an order of extension and separation basically similar to the one that managers have been calling explicate. By using the term 'thinking substances', in sharp contrast to the other, managers can infer clearly implying that the various distinct forms appearing in thought do not have their existence in such order of extension and separation, but rather in a different order in which extension and separations have no fundamental significances. The implicate order has just this latter quality and the managers may perhaps anticipate that conflict management has to be understood in terms of an order that is closer to the 'implicate' than it is to the 'explicate'. If sources of conflicts and the management of conflicts could in this way be understood together, in terms of the same general notion of order, the way would be opened to comprehending their relationship on the basis of some common ground. Thus we could come to the germ of a new notion of unbroken conflict management wholeness, in which managing the conflicts are no longer fundamentally separated from the organisational citizenship.

When a bio-psycho-social entity in a time and space (self) of organisational human unit, experience an imbalance due to certain determinable extraneous factors or of intergalactic intractabilities, it is mainly experienced as a conflict of ground-floor desires and the other pro-attitudes. The conflict arises due to reflective self evaluation and quest to regain the balance, in which some target-desire appears evaluatively undesirable to the person/s concerned. That desire or pro-attitude, howsoever compelling it may be, is concerned to be alien to oneself inasmuch as one prefers, on normative grounds to indentify oneself with a character or personality masks from which that desire or pro-attitude must be absent. Alienation of these characters that are naturally formed by ground floor desires and pro-attitudes combined with the underlying transactional stimulants prescribed by transactional theories thus forms a paradigm of being what they really want to be and that expressed as felt conflicts.

Contrastive characterisations of desires or motivations with its constructive/destructive multitudinal influentials are indicative of awareness of and sensitivity to qualitative depth of particular mode of life pattern. Managers are strong evaluators who defines desires contrastively and precisely because they seems to be motivated to cast themselves as persons of certain kind, to live a kind of organisational life shaped by virtues of courage, nobility, integrity, honour and so on.

These evaluative visions draw out for them a preferred mode of organisational life by virtue of qualitative reflection upon the desires and motivations which express and sustain an organisational life of that kind. The felt springs of actions with its conflictual interests matter to them, not so much because of the attraction-repulsion of their consummations, but in virtue of the quality of the kind of organisational life and the kind of character that these desires-conflicts syndromes belong to. Granted that the pertinent viewpoint is that of the reactive attitude when it comes to judging persons or situations, it does not imply that it is always impertinent to adopt the objective attitude and there by finding solutions for innumerous conflicts, whatsoever the human circumstances may be. On the contrary, the participant attitudes in conflictual situations sometimes tend to give place to non participant attitudes, especially when the moral mask of the person is understood to be incapable of participating in ordinary human relationships, whether because of being asymmetrically oriented or because of being much too deranged. This peculiar dimension stimulates to talk about the pertinence of adopting the objective attitude towards the normal and the mature as a way of taking refuge from say the strains of involvement in conflictual situations or simply out of intellectual curiosity.

By the vastness of its extent, the enormity of its achievement, the manner of its invasion of, and the patterns of the influence it has sought to exert over, organisational human life and conduct, the conflict management renders requisite and exigent a revaluation of its central conceptions, and a determination of the scope of its inquiries and the limitations of its techniques. When an organisational human interaction happens, human elements had to re-orientate their minds, to a large extent, particularly to an appreciable extent. Even against the surface-conscience there is an urge from within the depth of every being to find the eternal resonance with the organisations and their environment that they enjoy, whether this is felt perfectly or otherwise. The words of eternal knowledge and the experience shared   by management gurus are the ripe fruits of such fine flowers blossomed out in the light of the wisdom. They lead us to the efficient conflict management in organisations, which are but its psychological parts.

The differences among the conceptions regarding the efficacies of the various methods of the transformation and integration of individuals' efforts synchronised with that of the organisational into the higher consciousness (organisational developmental measures) are due to the varying temperaments and grades of experience of those individuals engaged in the task of comprehending the organisational understanding. Each of the ego-centers is different from the other in consciousness and experience. They require higher touches of experience varying in degree, in proportion to the subtlety of the condition of their present state of consciousness.

Management and organisation, likewise, is not an invention of human crotchet or an outcome of fear/greed or even a social necessity but the answer to a living surge of conscious aspiration which cannot be intelligible either to reason or to science. Human nature is not a combination of scientific facts alone or a bundle of physical laws or chemical elements, but manifests in itself a meaning higher than all observable values in the world of mathematics, physics, chemistry or biology. The spirit of management is different from the beaten track of logical philosophy, for it reads an eternal meaning in the temporal structure of the world. It is here that we come face to face with the fact that management is neither a predisposed practice nor a human contrivance but the perennial activity of timeless being and the trail to the universal resonance within. This important factor is forgotten by the modern organisational manager, however much educated he may be. He has refused to walk freely with the workings of the spiritual and integral nature and has attempted his best to centre himself in the state of individualised existence.

The misery of the present-day managerial conflicts and its inefficient management may be attributed to this constrictive tendency in the managers, which is ever trying to block the way of the expansion of the integral consciousness. The case of the half-baked material science and psychology may be specially mentioned here as being one of the forces obstructive to the happy process of Truth-realisation. The ills caused by wrong methods of education, the social and political strife, the individual evils and the world-degeneration are all effected by the one terrible fact that humanity has turned against the law of the spiritual reality. So long as this self-destructive tendency of the human mind is not controlled, and man is not shown the correct way of procedure, the unhappy world has to be contented with its fate. The remedy lies in our being sincere in taking recourse to the direct method of such realisation here and now. A manager has to be cent-per-cent integral.

Occasional and strategic departure from the reactive attitude to the objective/proactive attitude under special circumstances is itself rooted in the organisational citizens' inquest to break the box and make himself more creatively responsible by wearing the more constructive masks of his personality. This explains the possibility of transformative, resonential and other constructive approaches to manage the conflicts. The reactive attitude which defines the personal stance seems to override any switch-over to the complete objective/proactive attitude such that there is no genuine human possibility of our being entirely overtaken by the objective/proactive attitude without losing our human/self identity. This may well explain the usage of comparatively lower intensified transformative, resonential approaches than the elongated fight/flight attitude when it comes to manage conflicts in organisational spheres. The balancing acts of these attitudinal synergies are initiated by inculcating the value system and its various dynamic constituents like ethos, predominant prioritisations of desires, springs of actions, etc. Thus organisational citizens are such that their being is in question in their being. These person contingent features are various specific needs and desires, ways of perceiving things, moods and manners and many other dispositions, all of which make up the ground floor resources of ordinary organisational life with its prenotions of inculcated values and its management. Conflict managerial values represent an internal framework that has the potential to provide meaning to our lives and the way in which we lead them. Knowing and living by the conflict managerial values enriches managerial self-development and leads to an understanding of the purpose of our organisational lives. Conflict managerial values are helpful in maintaining the personal self-esteem in the face of challenge and disappointment. They are the principles by which managers may choose to live in the organisational world.

The idea of strong evaluation of conflict managerial values seems to be an undercurrent in many conflict theories of past– be it from Blake and Mouton, Thomas-Kilmann, Mary Parker Follett, Stephen Robbins, Johan Galtung or Thomas Weber. It seems to be perfectly theorised and put into practice by the likes of Mahatma Gandhi echoed out of ancient wisdom-consciousness of India. The values that inform the value-consciousness of the conflict manager must themselves be objective in the sense that if a value is not objectively there, it is difficult, nay, impossible that there be a value-consciousness at all in the most appropriate proactive situational response mode. The manager of conflicts presupposes the system of values which he is trained to imbibe and manifest in his judgements. The value system of him is rationally and consciously adopted after a process of critical evaluation. The values themselves have a unity and coherence which make them the values of specific value-framework. There is an organic unity which binds them into a system. It is the intrinsic among them which deserve to be central, while the rest can belong to the periphery of the systems enabling dissonance-resonance balancing acts for managing conflicts. Values are not person-centric in the sense an artifact is man-made, but they are deeply ingrained in the human-value-consciousness. For example, the values of non-violence and respect for life are ingrained in the higher order consciousness of human beings as it is the very bedrock of human existence.

Values are ideals which set the tones to manage the conflicts and inculcating them to the organisational citizenship itself is a proactive phenomenon exercised by the human workforce in every organisations. Furthermore springs of value wings spreads to every imaginable level, let be it – intra-individualistic, interpersonal, intragroup, intergroup, organisational-system-wide or to superfluous multitudinal stakeholders of an organisation operating with a value system in time and space thereby expanding the horizons of conflict management domains.

Organisational human beings are natural conflict managers and have the capacity for self-transcendence and the ability to recognise value in others. Their reflective self-transcendence and or transformative approaches to managing the conflicts is certainly a product of reason as was convincingly displayed by Mahatma Gandhi's understanding/ managing the conflicts. Reason gives the human beings the status of constructive conflict managers. It is only humans who recognise the trans-subjective values. The realisation that other beings value themselves as one values oneself and that; it is the same value that is valued by different organisational creatures may lead to the recognition of intrinsic values during conflict management exercises. Rationality, consciousness, self-consciousness, intelligence, a sense of the past and the future, the capacity to relate to other, concern for others are some of the features which an organisational human unit inherit and needs to strengthen the notions of accountability, responsibility, meaningfulness so as to be applied to them all. All these features are gradable and actual organisational units possess these elements in different proportions. The challenge lies in the selection and appropriation of the most suitable ways of explaining these notions from innumerable prenotions that management thinkers had and going to be. It indeed certainly is a distinct human activity with its quest in finding the best situational response. The solution of *One best way* notion, which seems to be consistently rejected by the managerial acumen in past; and in future, management thought may pave way for more integral, integrative yet transformative guided principles for managing the conflicts experienced exclusively by its human constituents echoed from Gandhian schools of wisdom, beautifully crafted from the essence of ancient Indian mind-wisdom-consciousness.

9.5 Measures to improve conflict dynamics

- Managers need to possess required skills to position themselves as leaders. These skill sets include shared and pragmatic vision, assertiveness, skills for conflict management, organisational commitment and adaptability.

- Managers need to address the conflicts; look at the relationships of psycho-social bonding; reflect themselves as more than logical in theory and be creative; should be the practitioner of the skills of diagnosis and communication.

- Managers who are helping people to feel secure, to learn from their own experience, to reach their own decisions and to become more mature and independent is greatly appreciated by the organisational circles.

- Conflict management skills and comfort in using a variety of conflict-handling modes may help middle level managers to develop a repertoire of conflict managerial skills that are essential in effectively managing the variety of conflict situations.

- Managing effectively conflicts in a unit/department requires using strategies to actively encourage subordinates to attempt to handle their own problems, communicating honestly and openly, ensuring clarity of responsibility of roles, creating policies and changing if needed, and being sensitive to others and offer support.

- One of the major challenge counted by practicing managers and other stakeholders of contemporary management ethos, is the expressive development of a body of theory to explain why organisational conflicts take the form they do, and why they/others behave as they do, including various stratum of the managerial responses towards conflict dynamics. This calls for the sharing of the knowledge regarding conflict management for common goodness and benefits. Various universities, business associations and research institutions can play a better role in this regard.

- Conflict managerial values are not person-centric in the sense an artifact is man-made, but they are deeply ingrained in the human-value-consciousness. The values of non-violence and respect for life are ingrained in the higher order consciousness of human beings as it is the very bedrock of human existence and need to be inculcated among the business managers.

- To become effectively and for appropriately managing conflict, middle level managers must understand the causal-effects, theories, approaches and strategies of conflict management.

- The interactionist view of conflict management has a broader scope than the traditional notions of unitary and pluralist perspectives and the same is to be promoted. Further this can be strengthened by inculcating the principles of integral and integrated conflict management. In this regard Gandhian approach along the lines of Win-Win and built upon life principles need to be actively promoted. Integrated approach as propagated by Mary Parker Follett and can be accrued from various sources of body of knowledge including ancient Indian scriptures need to be ascertained.

- The need to impart training with an exclusive focus on conflict management skill enhancement among the business managers seems to a pressing one. Guided conflict management modules for business managers can be a better suggestive measure and the same can be utilised for further enhancement. The critical factors to be considered for imparting conflict management training were identified and put forth as suggestive measures. Training for efficient and constructive conflict management can be imparted not only for the managers but also for executives, supervisors and even for common workers.

- Management thought may pave way for more integral, integrative yet transformative guided principles for managing the conflicts when all the constituents of managing the conflicts were taken into consideration. Current models, theories and approaches of conflict management need to be creatively utilised for the same as they possess vital links to understand the hidden aspects of conflict management from the past.

Managing conflicts with others can be enervating, tedious and exasperating but can become a fascinating challenge if and only if the manager shows his real mental stature, guts and forbearance during the process. In handling the conflict situation, much depends upon the strategy and the tactical inputs that are redeemed by the managers dealing with other human elements in the organisation.

It appears that two kinds of organised learning are involved in managerial dealing with the organisational life. One is phylogenetic learning, in the sense that during organisational evolution-both the individualistic as well as system wide operations evolving very sophisticated machinery for perceiving and making inferences about the real world. In other words an organisational citizen approaches conflict perception a priori. What is a priori for an individual is a posteriori for the organisational units like groups, departments etc.

The second kind of organisational learning involved in dealing with the world is ontogenetic learning, namely the lifelong acquisition of cultural, linguistic and scientific managerial knowledge. Thus the organisational members see the world through multiple pairs of glasses; some of them are inherited as part of physiological apparatus, others acquired from direct experiences as they proceed through organisational life. Interestingly, a priori and a posteriori are relative terms, thoroughly intertwined with the phylogenetic and ontogenetic processes. Presumed common biological-phylogenetic heritage is so vast that it may lead the organisational thinkers to believe that all the members think and perceive and function in the same ways, but of this there can be no certain proof. Further the ontogenetic ways expels this wrong perception and strengthens the possibilities of conflict to occur more within and with others from individualistic perspectives of every social unit-be it an individual, group or even organisations.

The quest to find solutions to all possible answers start by strategising the patterns and attempting to find the commonness underlying through the advocacies of various theories and the practical exposures. Modern conflict management theories from various domains of knowledge seem to be of greater use and their assimilative nature enables every potential researcher fetch himself to superior heights and consciousness. Be it from psycho dynamic theory, transactional analysis, and psychomotor-psychosocial theories, all are indicating the commonness which itself reveals in uncommon ways. It may even get strengthened by the inclusion of propulsive theories like game theory or organisational learning theory. Amalgamation, assimilation, integration and amassing the knowhow which we gained through various paths of wisdom are to be the keywords for the future conflict management theories. In organisational spheres, micro-meso as well macro scientific experimentative studies is the need of the hour, apart from diagnostic and or descriptive research on conflict management. Indian organisations can play a vital role in this regard as they are propounded in these principles. Presence of ancient wisdom with the latest technologies is the indomitable component of our business organisations. Psychometrics and extensions of the philosophy of the conflict management enriched by postulations like conflict management strings (SPTs) are going to be a challenge and much depends upon the creative appropriation of such important instrumental applications in this field. Structural and procedural ways are also to be explored in its highest levels including associative institutions, research organisations as well as governmental machineries. Though academic in its origin, the resultants of this study can act as in valuable inputs along with other dimensions for reframing, revaluing and refining conflict management studies at this juncture.

In organisational plane of operation, each manager's sense world is strictly private and not directly accessible to anyone else. That inexorable, absolute division between spheres of conflict consciousness and their total and impenetrable exclusion of each other is always organised chaotic, yet falls under the nature's law of management. In spite of all this, there is the possibility of some degree of communication between the individuals and a surprising degree of commonality in the pictures of the world they separately create. The logical lines of thinking and acting can carry the organisational thinkers only so far, they peter out at some point, but they do indicate something beyond even though they cannot carry to there. Thus it can be said that the notions of all conflict consciousnesses are really one and the organisational conflict management needs to address the conflict consciousness management in its ever widening umbrella.

Managers (especially middle level managers) represent the infinite dynamics among the organisational understanding. To equip themselves, they are required to consciously evolve their thoughts into the harmonious tunes of this universe. An integral experience necessitates an integral approach, a transformation of the integral personality. The differences among the conceptions regarding the efficacies of various methods of the transformation of managerial personality into the higher consciousness (essence of conflict management) are due to the varying temperaments and grades of experience of those engaged in the task of realising the organisational affiliations and in some way their own existence. Each of the ego-centers (human psyche) is different from the other in consciousness and experience. They require higher touches of experience varying in degree, in proportion to the subtlety of the condition of their present state of consciousness while bringing organisational profits.

Organisational destructions, back biting, obliteration, and annihilation is not the purpose of organisations. Growth, evolution, constructive activity, and purposeful movement towards the ultimate affiliation and attachment, is the aim of the modern organisation. Hence, there exists a need to share knowledge, feeling, emotion and work among organisational workforce. Managers need to discover themselves and others in its true spirit and that can be only happening if managers by way of the description of knowledge, will, emotion and action attempts to do so. It leads to the integral development of the humanistic collective psyche and to the synergetic goals in every organisational sphere of life can be achieved. It is here that this study comes face to face with the fact that managerial understandings of conflict management are not one time organisational practice nor human contrivances; but the perennial activity of integrated and integral as well as 360 degree conflict management.

Management gurus were quick to appreciate the necessity to appeal to the various sides of human nature and to alter the method of teaching in adjustment with this need. Reality and creation in business organisations are not to be regarded as two facts or problems to be encountered but two ways of witnessing the same thing. The managerial mind is composed not only of the rational powers but also the emotional and the instinctive elements which feel the presence and working of certain truths that rationality cannot explain adequately.

Contemporary understanding of conflict management necessitates the theorisation of the practice of conflict management. This research/academic study gives suggestive measures towards integral, integrated and interactionist approaches of conflict management. Conflict management string model evolved through this study and the training modules ascertained by need based analysis are all part of futuristic projection for enabling the assessment of the practice of conflict management among the managers.

To bring effective positive change among managers regarding conflict management, it requires accepting many transcending organisational practices than merely reading and talking about conflict managerial values. Managers need to consider practical ways of weaving them into the fabric of everyday actions in their respective organisations. The initial ingredients rendered towards in this direction should start with the likes such as - openness, truthful interactions, humane and process-centric, free from exploitations, integrative inclusiveness, reciprocal relating, integrative unity, law of the situation, cumulative responsibility, functional cooperation, etc. And certainly this list may not get constrained itself to a comparatively smaller research group of this study, but certainly may expand its wings to those unimaginable heights which are of made up to manage the dissonance-resonance balances in every spectrum of organisational life forms where managerial interventions are possible. Furthermore, the last word in conflict management is that there is no last word in conflict management.

References

Referential notes and other major works including the textual references are highlighted in this section. To enable a better communication of the most relevant components which was constantly referred throughout the present study, it would be most appropriate to present a list of selected referential components. Further, an exhaustive referential module in a way or other would bring more flimsiness to this section. Thus, present list only bears signs of advanced/sustained references and assumes the pre-worked basic textual and other references in the issues fundamental to the study points.

Alam, O. G., and Srivastava, R. 1981. Punctuality as a function of alienation and ego strength. *Perspectives in Psychological Researches*, 4(11): 29-31.

Allport, F. 1955. *Theories of perception and the concept of structure*. New York: Wiley.

Alper, S., Tjosvold, D., and Law, K.S. 2000. Conflict management, efficacy, and performance in organizational teams. *Personnel Psychology*, 53: 625-642.

Amabile, T. M. 1996. *Creativity in context* (2 Ed.). Boulder, CO: Westview.

Amason, A. C. 1996. Distinguishing the effects of functional and dysfunctional conflict on strategic decision making: Resolving a paradox for top management teams. *Academy of Management Journal*, 39(1): 123-148.

Amason, A. C., and Sapienza, H. J. 1997. The effects of top management team size and interaction norms on cognitive and affective conflict. *Journal of Management* (23): 495-516.

Ansari.M. 1990. *Managing people at work: leadership styles and influence strategies*. New Delhi: Sage Publications.

Argote, L., Gruenfeld, D. H., and Naquin, C. 2001. Group learning in organizations. In M. E. Turner (Ed.), *Groups at Work: Advances in Theory and Research*: 369-411. Mahwah, NJ: Lawrence Erlbaum.

Argyris,C. 1964. *Integrating the individual and organization*. New York: Wiley.

Argyris,C. 1970. *Intervention Theory & Method: A Behavioral Science View*: Addison-Wesley.

Argyris, C. 1971. *Management and Organization Development*. New York: McGraw-Hill.

Athreya, M. B. 1997. Business Values for the 21st Century: HRM. *The New Frontiers*, 3(3): 7–10.

Axelrod, R. 1984. *The Evolution of Cooperation*. New York: Basic Books.

Babu, T. 2004. *A study on Conflict Resolution in Industrial Disputes – A Gandhian Approach*. Unpublished PhD Thesis: Gandhigram Rural Institute, India.

Bandura, A. 1977. Self-efficacy: Toward a unifying theory of behavioral change. *Psychological Review*, 84: 191-215.

Bandura, A. 1986. *Social foundation of thought and action: Social Theory*. Englewood Cliffs, N.J: Prentice Hall.

Barbara, B., and Rubin, J. Z. 1995. *Conflict, Cooperation & Justice*. Palo Alto: Jossey-Bass.

Barlingay, S. S. 1966. *A Modern Introduction to Indian Ethics*. New Delhi: Penman Publishers.

Barnett, M. E. 1990. The Relationship Between Personality Type and Choice of Conflict Resolution Mode. *Dissertation Abstracts International*, 51(5): 1504-A.

Baron, R. A. 1984. Reducing organizational conflict: An incompatible response approach. *Journal of Applied Psychology* (69): 272-279.

Ben-Yoav, O., and Banai, M. 1992. Measuring conflict management styles: A comparison between the MODE and ROCI–II instruments using self and peer ratings. *International Journal of Conflict Management*, I (3): 237–247.

Berk, R. A. 2003. *Regression analysis: A constructive critique*. Thousand Oaks, CA: Sage Publications.

Berkowitz, L. 1982. Aversive conditions as stimuli to aggression. In L. Berkowitz (Ed.), *Advances in Experimental Social Psychology*, Vol. 15: 249-288. New York: Ac. Press.

Berkowitz, L. 1993. *Aggression: Its Causes, Consequences and Control*. Philadelphia, PA: Temple University.

Bhaskar, K. R., and Mehrotra, A. . 1998. Managerial Values: A Study of Selected Organisations in India. *Personnel Today*, 18(4): 29–34.

Bies, R. J. 1987. The predicament of injustice: The management of moral outrage. *Research in Organizational Behavior* (9): 289-319.

Blake, R. A., and Mouton, J.S. 2006. *The New Managerial Grid*. New Delhi: Jaico Publications.

Blake, R. R., and Mouton, J.S. 1964. *The Managerial Grid*. Houston: Gulf Publishing Co.

Blake, R. R., Mouton, J.S., and Shepard, H.A. 1964. *Managing Intergroup Conflict in Industry*. Houston: Gulf Publishing Co.

Boryshenko, J. 1993. *Fire in the soul: A new psychology of spiritual optimism*. New York, NY: Warner Books, Inc.

Boulding, K. E. 1962. *Conflict and defense: a general theory*. New York: Harper & Brothers.

Boulding, K. E. 1963. Conflict Management as a Key to Survival. *American Journal of Orthopsychiatry*, 33(2): 230-231.

Bower, G. H., and Forgas, J. P. (Ed.). 2001. *Mood and social memory*. Mahwah, NJ: Lawrence Erlbaum Associates.

Brett, J. M., Shapiro, D. L., and Lytle, A. L. 1998. Breaking the bonds of reciprocity in negotiations. *Academy of Management Journal* (41): 410-424.

Brewer, M. B. 1996. When contact is not enough: Social identity and intergroup cooperation. *International Journal of Intercultural Relations* (20): 291-303.

Burton, J. W. 1997. *Violence Explained: The Sources of Conflict, Violence and Crime and their Prevention*. Manchester: Manchester University Press.

Bush, R. A. B., and Folger, J. P. 1994. *The promise of mediation: Responding to conflict through empowerment and recognition*. San Francisco, CA: Jossey-Bass.

Byrne, D. 1971. Attitudes and Attraction. In L.Berkowitz (Ed.), *Advances in Experimental and Social Psychology*. New York, NY: Academic Press.

Chakrabarty, S. 2002. Evaluation of Rahim's Organizational Conflict Inventory as a measure of conflict-handling styles in a sample of Indian salespersons. *Psychological Reports*, 90: 549-567.

Church, A. H., and McMahan, G.C. 1995. Key Characteristics of OD in Rapidly Growing Firms. *ASTD OD Newsletter*, Fall/Winter: 7–8.

Churchman, D. 2005. *Why We Fight: Theories of Human Aggression and Conflict*. Lanham, MD: University Press of America.

Cohen, H. 1980. *You Can Negotiate Anything*. Secaucus, NJ: Lyle Stuart.

Cornelius, H., and Shoshana, Faire. 1989. *Everyone Can Win: How to Resolve Conflict*. Sydney: Simon & Schuster.

Cosier, R., and Rose, G. 1977. Cognitive conflict and goal conflict effects on task performance. *Organizational Behavior and Human Decision Processes* (19): 378-391.

Crawley, J. 1992. *Constructive Conflict Management: Managing to Make a Difference*: Nicholas Bealey Publishing.

Dalton, E. M. 1979. *Management: foundations and practices* (5ed.).New York: McMillan Press

Das, G. S. 1987. Conflict management styles of efficient branch managers: As perceived by others. *ASCI Journal of Management*, 17(1): 30–38.

Dayal, I. 1970. *New concepts in management*. Bombay: Lalvani Publishing House.

Dayal, I. 2002. Group and intergroup relations. *Indian Journal of Industrial Relations*, 37(4).

De Dreu, C. K. W., Nauta, A., and Van de Vliert, E. 1995. Self-serving evaluations of conflict behavior and dispute. *Journal of Applied Social Psychology*, 25(23): 2049-2066.

Denzin, N., K. and Yvonna, Lincoln. 2003. *Strategies of qualitative inquiry* (2 ed.). Thousand Oaks, CA: Sage Publications.

Deutsch, M., and Robert M. Krauss. 1960. Effect of Threat on Interpersonal Bargaining. *Journal of Abnormal and Social Psychology* 61(2): 181–189.

Dollard, J. 1980. *Frustration and Aggression*. Westport, CT: Greenwood.

Donohue, W. A. 1992. *Managing Interpersonal Conflict*: Sage.

Druckman, D. 2005. *Doing Research: Methods of Inquiry for Conflict Analysis*. Thousand Oaks: Sage.

Dwivedi, R. S. 1981. *Dynamics of Human Behaviour at Work*. New Delhi: Oxford and IBH Publishing Company.

Dwivedi, R. S. 2001. *Human relations and organisational behaviour*. New Delhi: Macmillan India ltd.

Eisenhardt, K. M., Jean L. Kahwajy, and., Bourgeois, L .J. III. 1997. How management teams can have a good fight. *Harvard Business Review*, 75(4): 77–85.

Fernandez, G., Pattanayak, Dhar, Ravishankar. 2000. *For one and all Human skills*. New Delhi: Himalaya Publishing House.

Finkelstein, S. 2003. *Why smart executives fail*. New York: Portfolio.

Fisher, R., and Ury, William. 1987. *Getting to Yes: Negotiating Agreement Without Giving In* (2 ed.). London: Arrow.

Follett, M. P. 1924. *Creative Experience*. London: Longmans.

Forgas, J. P. 1995. Mood and judgment: The affect infusion model (AIM). *Psychological Bulletin* (117): 39-66.

Fraser, N., and Hipel, K. 1984. *Conflict Analysis: Models and Resolutions*. Amsterdam: Elsevier Science.

French, W. L., and Bell, C.H. 1973. *Organization Development: Behavioural Science Interventions for Organizational Improvement* Englewood Cliffs, N.J: Prentice-Hall.

Frey, L. R. (Ed.). 1995. *Innovations in Group Facilitation*. New Jersey: Hampton Press.

Friedman, R. A., Tidd, S.T., Currall, S.C., and Tsai, J.C. 2000. What goes around comes around: The impact of personal conflict style on work conflict and stress. *International Journal of Conflict Management*, 11: 32-55.

Fryman, S. 2006. *The Psychology of Prejudice*. New York: Penguin Publications.

Fucilla, R. 2001. *The influence of cultural and individual level variables on conflict avoidance behavior: A cross-cultural study of U.S. and Latin American professionals*. Unpublished Master's thesis, University of Wisconsin-Milwaukee.

Gandhi, M. K. 1900. *Fellowship of faiths and unity of religions*. New Delhi: GB House.

Gandhi, M. K. 1940. *An Autobiography or The Story of My Experiments With Truth*. Ahmedabad: Navajivan.

Gandhi, M. K. 1932-36. Editorial and other selected articles, *Harijan*.

Gandhi, M. K. 1959. *The message of the Gita*. Ahmedabad: Navajivan.

Gandhi, M. K. 2000. *Thought for the day*. New Delhi: Publication Division, Ministry of Information and Broadcasting, Government of India.

Gangadhara, R., and Surya, P. Rao. 1996. *The Dynamics of Group Behaviour*. New Delhi: Kanishka Publishers.

Gangrade, K. D. 1998. *Gandhi's Autobiography: Moral lessons*. New Delhi: Gandhi smriti and darshan samiti, Rajghat.

Gangrade, K. D., Kothari, L.S., and Verma, A.R. 2005. *Concept of truth in Science and Religion*. New Delhi: Gandhi Smriti and Darshan Samiti, Rajghat.

Ganguli, B. N. 2000. *Gandhi's social philosophy, perspective and relevance*. New Delhi: National Gandhi Museum.

George, R., and David, Walchak. 1986. *Working: Conflict and Change* (3 ed.). New Delhi: Prentice Hall.

Ghosh, D. 1993. Risk propensity and conflict behavior in dyadic negotiation: Some evidence from the laboratory. *International Journal of Conflict Management*, 4: 223–247.

Goel, S. L. 2000. *Modern management techniques*. New Delhi: Deep and Deep Publications.

Gottshalk, J. 2002. *Crisis Management*. New York: John Wiley and Sons.

Gross, M. A., and Guererro, L. K. 2000. Managing conflict appropriately and effectively: An application of the competence model to Rahim's organizational conflict styles. *International Journal of Conflict Management*, 11(3): 200-226.

Hall, L. (Ed.). 1993. *Negotiation: Strategies for Mutual Gain*: Sage.

Hammond, J. S., Keeney, R.L., and H. Raiffa. 1999. *Smart choices: A practical guide to making better decisions*. Harvard: HBS Press.

Hingorani, A., T. (Ed.). 1971. *Teaching of the Gita, Gandhi*. Bombay: Bharathiya Vidya Bhawan.

Holman, D. J., and Wall, T.J. 2002. Work Characteristics, Learning-Related Outcomes, and Strain: A Test of Competing Direct Effects, Mediated, and Moderated Models. *Journal of Occupational Health Psychology* (7): 283-301.

Husain, A., S. 1969. *Gandhiji and communal unity*. New Delhi: Orient Longman.

Janis, I. L. 1997. Groupthink. In R. L. Vecchio (Ed.), *Leadership: Understanding the dynamics of power and influence in organizations*: 163-176. Notre Dame, IN: University of Notre Dame Press.

Jehn, K. A. 1995. A multimethod examination of the benefits and detriments of intragroup conflict. *Administrative Science Quarterly* (40): 256-282.

Jehn, K. A. 1997. A qualitative analysis of conflict types and dimensions in organizational groups. *Administrative Science Quarterly* (42): 530-557.

Jehn, K. A., and Mannix, E. A. 2001. The dynamic nature of conflict: A longitudinal study of intragroup conflict. *Academy of Management Journal* (44): 238-251.

Joseph P. Folger.Scott, M., Poole., and Randall, K. Stutman. 1996. *Working through Conflict: Strategies for Relationships, Groups and Organizations* (3 ed.): Harper-Collins.

Joshi, K. 2002. *Philosophy of value-oriented education: theory and practice.* New Delhi: Indian Council of Philosophical Research.

Katzenbach, J. R., and Smith, D. K. 1993. The discipline of groups. *Harvard Business Review*, March-April, 71(2): 111-120.

Kautilya. 1912. Arthashastra. In T. Ganapathi Sastrigal (Ed.), Vol. 1-3. Mysore: Mysore Oriental Library.

Kay, E. 1974. *The crisis in middle management.* New York: Amacom.

Kilmann, R. H., and Thomas,K. W. 1982. Four Perspectives on Conflict Management: An Attributional Framework for Organizing Descriptive and Normative Theory. In V. J. Kelly and Baba (Ed.), *The New Management Scene*. Englewood Cliffs, NJ: Prentice-Hall.

Kissinger, H. 1994. *Diplomacy*. New York: Simon & Schuster.

Kothari, C. R. 2006. *Research Methodology* (2 ed.). New Delhi: Wishwa Prakashan.

Kruskal, J. B., and Wish, M. 1978. *Multidimensional scaling*. Beverly Hills, CA: Sage.

Kurtz, E., and Ketcham, K. 1993. *The spirituality of imperfection*. NY: Bantam Books.

Laird, W. M., and Gary,P.Latham. 1996. *Skills for managerial success-theory,experience and practice*: Irwin Publications.

Lallan, P., and Banerjee,A.M. 1981. *Management of Human Resources*. Jaipur: Sterling Publishers.

Lawley, D. N., and Maxwell, A. E. 1971. *Factor analysis as a statistical method*. London: Butterworth and Co.

Levitt, S., and Steven, Dubner. 2005. *Freakonomics*. New York: William Morrow.

Lewicki, R. J., Saunders, D. M., Minton, J. W., and Barry, B. 2002. *Negotiation: Readings, exercises, and cases*. New York: McGraw-Hill/Irwin.

Lipman-Blumen, J., and Leavitt, H. J. 1995. Hot groups. *Harvard Business Review*, July-August 73(4).

Lorenz, K. 1974. *On Aggression*. New York: Harvest.

Louis, E. B., and David,L.Kurtz. 1992. *Management*. New York: McGraw Hill Inc.

Luthans, F. 1998. *Organisational Behaviour* (8 International ed.). New York: McGraw-Hill.

Machiavelli, N. 1513, 2003. *The Prince*. London: Penguin.

Maitra, S. K. 1963. *The Ethics of the Hindus*. Kolkata: Calcutta University Press.

Maslow, A. H. 1954. *Motivation and personality* (2 ed.). New York: Harper & Row.

Mathur, H. B., and Sayeed,O.B. 1990. Application of conflict management strategies as perceived by the manager for himself and for his supervisor. *Indian Journal of Social Works*, 41(2): 163-169.

McGrath, J. E. 1984. *Groups: Interaction and performance*. Englewood Cliffs, NJ: Prentice Hall.

McKenna, E. 2000. *Business psychology and Organisational Behaviour* (Students' ed.). New York: Taylor and Francis Inc.

McWhorter, J. 2005. *Winning the Race*. New York: Penguin.

Mills, R. D., and Smith,L. 1985. Conflict handling and personality dimensions of project management personnel. *Psychological Reports*, 57(3): 1135-1143.

Narayan, B., and Sharma,Bharathi. 2004. *Behavioural science in management*. New Delhi: Omsons Publications.

Nicotera, A. M., Smilowitz,M. and Pearson,J.C. 1990. Ambiguity tolerance, conflict management style and argumentativeness as predictors of innovativeness. *Communication Research Reports*, 7(2): 125-131.

Nizam al-Mulk. ca 1095, 1978. *Siyasatnama (The Book of Government or Rules for Kings)*. London: Routledge.

Pelled, L. H. 1996. Demographic diversity, conflict, and work group outcomes: An intervening process theory. *Organization Science*(7): 615-631.

Pinkley, R. L. 1990. Dimensions of conflict frame: Disputant interpretations of conflict. *Journal of Applied Psychology*, 75: 117-126.

Porter, M. 1998. *Competitive Strategy*. New York: The Free Press.

Rahim, M. A., and Bonoma, T.V. 1979. Managing organizational conflict: a model for diagnosis and intervention. *Psychological Reports*(44): 1323-1344.

Rahim, M. A. 1980. Some contingencies affecting interpersonal conflict in academia: A multivariate study. *Management International Review*, 20(2): 117–121.

Rahim, M. A. 1983. A measurement of styles of handling interpersonal conflict. *Academy of Management Journal*(26): 368-376.

Rahim, M. A. 1997. Styles of managing organizational conflict: A critical review and synthesis of theory and research. In R. T. G. M. A. Rahim, and L. E. Pate (Ed.), *Current topics in management*, Vol. 2: 61–77. Greenwich, CT: JAI Press.

Rahim, M. A. 2001. Managing organizational conflict: Challenges for organization development and change. In R. T. Golembiewski (Ed.), *Handbook of organizational behavior*, 2 ed.: 365–387. New York: Marcel Dekker.

Raiffa, H. 1982. *Art and Science of Negotiation*. Cambridge: Harvard University.

Rapoport, A. 1960. *Fights. Games and Debates*. Ann Arbor, MI: University of Michigan Press.

Richard E. Walton, Joel, Cutcher-Gershenfeld., and Robert, B. McKersie. 1994. *Strategic Negotiations : A Theory of Change in Labor-Management Relations*. Boston: HBS

Robbins, S. P. 1974. *Managing Organizational Conflict: A Non-Traditional Approach*. Englewood Cliffs, N.J: Prentice-Hall.

Robbins, S. P. 1998. *Organisational Behaviour*. New Delhi: Prentice Hall of India Pvt.Ltd.

Robbins, S. P. 1998. *Organization theory structure,design and applications* (3 ed.). New Delhi: Prentice Hall of India.

Robert, A. B., Donn Byrne, Blair,T.Johnson. 1998. *Exploring Social Psychology* (4 ed.): Allyn and Bacon Publishers.

Robert, B. L., and Zhengsen. 1998. *Organisational Psychology-foundations and applications*. London: Oxford University Press.

Roger Fisher, E. K., and Andrea Kupfer Schneider. 1994. *Beyond Machiavelli : Tools for Coping with Conflict*. Cambridge, Mass: Harvard University Press.

Rogers, C. 1961. *On Becoming a Person: A Therapist's View of Psychotherapy*. Boston, MA: Houghton Mifflin.

Ross, L., and., Nisbett, R. E. 1991. *The person and the situation: Perspectives of social psychology*. Philadelphia: Temple University Press.

Ross, R. 1989. Conflict. In R. Ross, and Ross,J. (Ed.), *Small groups in organizational settings*: 139-178. Englewood Cliffs, NJ: Prentice Hall.

Roy, D. 1997. Values in Management: Present Scene and Future Needs. *Management Accountant*, 32(8): 592–596.

Saiyaddhin, M. S. 1988. *Human Resources Management*. New Delhi: Tata McGraw-Hill.

Samantara, R. 2003. Management of superior-subordinate conflicts: an exploration. *Indian Journal of Industrial Relations*, 38(4).

Samantara, R. 2004. Conflict management strategies and organisational effectiveness. *Indian Journal of Industrial Relations*, 39(3).

Sayeed, O. B. 1990. Conflict management styles: relationship with leadership styles and effect of esteem for coworker. *Indian Journal of Industrial Relations*, 26(3): 227-243.

Sayeed, O. B. 1993. Leadership effectiveness and managerial response to conflict strategies. *Productivity*, 34(1): 99-108.

Schein, E. H. 1992. *Organizational culture and leadership*. San Francisco: Jossey-Bass Publishers.

Schellenberg, J. A. 1996. *Conflict Resolution: Theory, Research, and Practice*. Albany: State University of New York.

Schneider, B. 1985. Organizational Behavior. *Annual Review of Psychology*, 36: 573-611.

Schweiger, D. M. 1989. A meta-analysis on the comparative effectiveness of devil's advocacy and dialectical inquiry. *Strategic Management Journal*(10): 303-306.

Schwenk, C. R. 1990. Conflict in organizational decision making: An exploratory study of its effects in for-profit and not-for-profit organization. *Management Science*, 36(4): 436-448.

Shapiro, D. L., and Rosen, B. 1994. An investigation of managerial interventions in employee disputes. *Employee Responsibilities and Rights Journal*, 7(1): 53-72.

Sharp, G. 1999. *Gandhi as political strategist, with Essays on ethics and politics.* (Indian ed.). New Delhi: Gandhi media centre.

Sherif, M. 1967. *Group Conflict and Cooperation: Their Special Psychology*. London: Routledge, Kegan Paul.

Silva, M. O. S. 2000. *Conflict source and conflict management style at Notre Dame of Greater manila as perceived by grade school and high school administrators and teachers, school year 1998-1999*. Unpublished Master's thesis, Ateneo De Manila University, Philippines.

Simmel, G. 1955. *Conflicts*. New York: The Free Press.

Simons, T. L., and Peterson, R. S. 2000. Task conflict and relationship conflict in top management teams: The pivotal role of intergroup trust. *Journal of Applied Psychology*(85): 102-112.

Thomas, K. W., and Kilmann, R. H. 1974. *The Thomas-Kilmann conflict mode instrument*. Tuxedo, NY: Xicom.

Thomas, K. W., and Kilmann, R. H. 1977. Developing a Forced-Choice Measure of Conflict-Handling Behavior: The "Mode" Instrument. *Educational and Psychological Measurement*, 37(2): 309-325.

Ting-Toomey, S. 1997. Intercultural conflict competence. In D. W. Cupach and Canary (Ed.), *Competence in interpersonal conflict*: 120-147. New York: McGraw-Hill.

Tjosvold, D. 1985. Implications of controversy research for management. *Journal of Management Science*(11): 21-37.

Tjosvold, D. 1997. Conflict within interdependence: Its value for productivity and individuality. In C. K. W. D. D. a. E. V. d. Vliert (Ed.), *Using Conflict in Organizations*, 2 ed.: 651-717. Palo Alto, CA: Consulting Psychologists Press.

Ury, W. 1991. *Getting Past No: Negotiating with Difficult People*. New York: Bantam Books.

Van de Vliert, E., and Kabanoff, B. 1990. Toward theory-based measures of conflict management. *Academy of Management Journal*, 33: 199–209.

Van de Vliert, E. 1997. *Complex interpersonal behavior: Theoretical frontiers*. Hove, UK: Psychology Press.

Venkaiah, V., and Rao,V.S.P. 1991. Organisational conflicts: concepts,models,types and resolution strategies. In V. S. P. Rao (Ed.), *Organisation Development*: 3-41. New Delhi: Discovery Publishing House.

Verma, R. 2001. *The spiritual basis of satyagraha*. Ahmedabad: Navajivan Publishing House.

Weber, T. 1992. *Gandhian way of conflict resolution*. New Delhi: Gandhi peace foundation.

Weber, T. 2001. Gandhian Philosophy, Conflict Resolution Theory and Practical Approaches to Negotiation. *Journal of Peace Research*, 38(4): 493–513.

Weider-Hatfield, D. 1988. Assessing the Rahim Organizational Conflict Inventory–II (ROCI–II). *Management Communication Quarterly*, 1: 350–366.

Weider-Hatfield, D., and Hatfield, J. D. 1995. Relationships among conflict management styles, levels of conflict, and reactions to work. *Journal of Social Psychology*(135): 687-699.

Welch, J. 2001. *Jack: Straight from the gut*. New York: Warner Business Books.

Wilkinson, L., Blank,G. and Gruber,C. 1996. *Desktop Data Analysis* Upper Saddle River, NJ: Prentice-Hall.

William Baskaran, M. 2004. *Indian Perspectives on Conflict Resolution*. Thiruvananthapuram: Gandhi Media Centre.

Wilmot, W., and Joyce, L. Hocker. 2005. *Interpersonal Conflict*. New York: McGraw-Hill.

Wittenbaum, G. M., and Stasser, G. 1996. *Management of information in small groups*. Thousand Oaks, CA: Sage Publications.

Wittenbaum, G. M., Hollingshead, A. B. et al. 2004. From cooperative to motivated information sharing in groups: Moving beyond the hidden profile paradigm. *Communication Monographs*, 71(3): 286-310.

Wolfe D. M.and Kolb, D. A. 1980. Beyond specialization: the quest for integration in midcareer. In N. C. Derr (Ed.), *Work, family and career*. New York, NY: Praeger.

Worchel, S., and Simpson, J.A. (Ed.). 1997. *Conflict between People and Groups*. Chicago: Nelson-Hall Publishers.

Xie, J., Michael Song,X. and Anne Stringfellow. 1998. Interfunctional Conflict, Conflict Resolution Styles, and New Product Success: A Four-Culture Comparison. *Management Science*, 44(12): 192-206.

Zhou, J., and George, J. M. 2001. When job dissatisfaction leads to creativity: Encouraging the expression of voice. *Academy of Management Journal*, 44(4): 682-696.